Praise for 9

"In this book, Donovan and colleagues invite teachers to rethink the teaching of poetry and to reimagine it as relational, as community building, and as anti-oppressive. Full of practical steps and insight, 90 Ways of Community walks readers through the processes of setting up notebooks and establishing procedures to the day-by-day plans for making poetry part of the classroom culture."

~**Mike Cook**, Auburn University author of *Exploring Relationships and Connection to Others: Teaching Universal Themes through Young Adult Literature*

"Educators looking for practical strategies for teaching poetry will find what they need in this stunningly powerful text. This book invites teachers and students to engage in conversation through daily writing activities. With an emphasis on poetry as a transactional and empathy-building experience, *90 Ways of Community* dovetails well with Nancie Atwell or Jim Burke's writing workshop models."

~**Kia Jane Richmond**, Northern Michigan University author of *Mental Illness in Young Adult Literature: Exploring Real Struggles through Fictional Characters*

"This book, with its collection of prompts, mentor poems, and practical tools, will help teachers move poetry out of the shadows of a single unit and into the daily work we do to help students explore their inner and outer worlds and leverage it as a tool to nurture and heal. We know that poetry holds immeasurable power, and this book will help us share that power with our students."

~**Erin Vogler,** English Teacher and Literacy Coach, Keshequa Central School, NY

More Praise for 90 Ways of Community

"Grounded by a National Writing Project ethos, this book showcases teacher writing and teacher practice. It is a useful resource for teachers who want to infuse poetry writing into their classrooms in order to elevate student voice."

~**Kristen Turner**, Drew University recipient of the ELATE/NCTE Richard A. Meade Award

"Poetry, the magical unit when students are most excited to write, I am most excited to read their writing, and they're most engaged with one another. Maureen, Mo, and Sarah provide an easy method to ensure poetry magic happens all school year long. I can't wait to incorporate this book into my lesson plans!"

~**Tracie McCormick**, Middle School Administrator and 8th grade teacher

90 Ways of Community

Nurturing Safe & Inclusive Classrooms
Writing One poem at a Time

Sarah J. Donovan

Mo Daley

Maureen Young Ingram

Made possible by the writers of the Ethical ELA Community

Seela Books
Stillwater, OK 74075
www.ethicalela.com

ISBN: 978-0-9998768-4-8

Editor: Sarah J. Donovan

For the poet within us all

Contents

Introduction to Poetic Community Building

A Poetic Story

An ELA teacher reflected on their successful April poetry unit and how there was a positive energy in the room as students explored diverse writers and poetry styles. Each day, the teacher set aside time for quiet writing, followed by partner sharing, poetry read-alouds, and Friday poetry slams. Students declared poetry as their favorite writing of the year, and the teacher echoed this praise, adding that one of the most surprising finds was the effect of this writing on his most challenging student. This young man, let's call him 'Paul,' had pushed boundaries all year long with teachers, classmates, and his family. Paul seemed discontented with school in general. Yet, the daily poetry writing spoke to Paul, flipping a switch on his discordant behavior, and resulting in him writing with focus and passion. The teacher wondered what made this writing so appealing. Was it the loosening of rules that poetry offers - the ability to write freely, from the heart? Without a doubt, the student was centered by this work, and this positivity seemed to carry him through his day.

Why did poetry writing work as well as it did for Paul? Paul didn't have the term for it and the teacher likely didn't either, but what Paul and his teacher had been doing was a simple, often-limited-to-April version of relational poetic writing. Paul's poetry changed how he felt about writing, how he felt about school, who he knew he was (a poet), and it changed his relationship with both his teacher and classmates. The teacher, in turn, discovered something about Paul and what he needed to be centered and able to engage with others in a way that made learning come alive. And now, it's this approach to teaching writing that could help save countless youth from turning from writing and being writers to use their voices, to shape their lives, and to contribute to the words that go into their worlds. Relational poetry could save traditional writing instruction from itself.

What Poetic Writing Is, What This Book Is (and Isn't)

Maybe hearing that writing poetry could change everything you've experienced as a writing teacher is a little intense or off-putting. We haven't even explained what relational poetic writing even is and why this topic matters in the first place. We promise not to be so grandiose throughout this book, but we also think it is important not to understate the transformative possibilities in daily poetic writing practices. So, with that in mind, let's consider what relational poetic writing is and what you are getting yourself into with this book.

While a detailed explanation of relationality and relational and poetry and writing and all the benefits take up the next chapter, here is a very brief definition that might prove helpful at the start: if you are inviting students to write poetry about themselves, their families, the community, the world, the future, you are engaging in some form of relational poetic writing.

Let's look at the definition in the context of Paul's story. The act of asking students to write a poem is as simple as opening a notebook (or even having a notebook), using class time to actually write (rather than assigning something for homework), and writing a list of where they're from (the products, places, people). This freedom from too many rules or points managed to be what Paul was looking for his entire school career.

He had to make several choices:

- his audience (the teacher, classmates, family),
- how he'd use the white space on the page to organize his thoughts,
- choose words very precisely in this concentrated form,
- trust the reader to infer what rested in the blank spaces,
- reflect on what was most essential and defining for him while also
- trusting in the power of specifics to reach other's minds, and

2

- draw on his life for content that was only partially dependent on a text offered to him not as "the right way" but as a mentor or partner poet (George Ella Lyon) to encourage his ideas.

Only Paul could have written that poem, and he wanted to write it. The poem gave Paul a purpose, a path, a witness, and an identity that he claimed in the writing of that poem. The activity asked him to look at school, at English language arts, at his ELA teacher, at his ELA classmates in ways he had never previously considered. Maybe Paul had written other poems, but this was the time he noticed a poetic way of being – a gentleness with himself, a figurative presence that found poetry in him. Writing poetry during April or having a fun activity one day to write a poem may surface some joy and poetic thinking, but over time, poetic engagements have the power to alter the culture of a classroom, the writing identities of students, and the way a teacher interacts with students. Relational poetic practice is about writing, but it is also about school culture. You may call it classroom management, but we call it poetry in motion.

So, if that's what relational poetic writing is and what it can do (at least in this brief introductory form), what exactly can you expect in this book? To begin, this isn't the place for a lot of theory. Okay, we will dig into it a bit in the next chapter, but after that, every page will be a poetic practice for you to use as is or adapt in your classroom. Theory is really important because it is grounding in practice. Without knowing why you are doing something, you run the risk of plug-and-play or skills-based only or checking boxes – and soon enough you recognize the Pauls in your classroom are lost, uninspired, asking for a reason to care. In Sarah's workshops with teacher-leaders, she shares a framework for pedagogy that is grounded in the National Council of Teachers of English's teacher preparation standards, and that is 1) a youth lens that believes deeply in the ability now for students to make decisions and direct their learning and 2) inclusive-affirming curriculum that shows students cultures, languages, identities in the texts, images, and assignments so that they are part of the curriculum.

Theory matters, but we know teachers need something they can use now. Today. With increasing numbers of emergency-certified teachers entering schools, we know teachers are looking for something that will help them become teachers (you will always be becoming) and do no harm in the process. We think this book will help you repair past harms that may make students hate writing or hate poetry – red marks on their papers, jeers from peers, misguided focus on correctness. The books that we have found most helpful in our own practice and that Sarah has used with her preservice teachers are ones like Beers and Probst's *Notice and Note: Strategies for Close Reading* (2012) and Gallagher and Kittle's *180 Days: Two Teachers and the Quest to Engage and Empower Adolescents* (2018). These books have how-to surrounded by why and insider tips from their actual practice in actual classrooms.

So this is not a book about poetry theory or even about poets. There aren't even any poems by the poets that likely come to mind when you think of writing poetry – those war poets or ones in movies like "Do Not Go Gentle" by Dylan Thomas in *Dangerous Minds* or "Oh, Captain, My Captain" in *Dead Poets Society*. We are not going to talk too much about reading poetry or poets – other than the poets in your classroom. This is about them and their writing.

So, yes, that's it. What this book is about is your students, their writing, and, perhaps more importantly, their writing daily over time together with you. This book is a resource for you.

Who is this book for?

It is that how–to practical book that you can rely on as you start your class each day, every day, for 180 days. It is one thing you can depend on and that your students can depend on. Their notebook will be waiting for them each day with a new blank page welcoming a poem written by their hand, not a worksheet they fill in (unless this is an accommodation, which can be pasted in the notebook). They will make blank pages sing with their lives, and in sharing these with one another, your classroom and their lives will be forever different. If you have never had a group of friends who were poets, if you have never been in a room with poets, then you may be skeptical, but after a few weeks of writing poetry together, you will feel it and know we are right.

Community Building with Poetry: Relationality

What sets this book apart from other texts with poetry prompts is the relational angle we've tried to take, along with the insider tips about how to move through each lesson that is often missing from other poem books or writing prompt books. You have many, many years of experience with the teachers who have written this book you are holding. We have written every poem we recommend you write; we have written poetry with our students for years; we have shared poetry with parents, communities, and the nation. We have sat at tables at national and international conferences with teachers to share lessons and discoveries about writing poetry with students.

What we have found missing from many of the poetry prompt books is the process. The moves a teacher makes with their bodies and voices; the moves the teacher makes to bring students into conversation and community – those are not in the other books. Many of those books were written by one author - more often a poet, sometimes a teacher – but not always someone who knows what it means to teach 6 classes and 180 students every day all school year for decades. Experienced teachers know how essential it is for the classroom to be a place of belonging and engagement, for students to be seen and heard. We have used many of the poetry anthologies and poetry prompts, but these do not translate or transfer well to new teachers or teachers who do not already like or want to like writing poetry. And above all, what seems to be missing from almost every professional conversation about writing and English language arts more broadly is poetry writing in secondary classrooms. Reading is and always has been the center. Canonical texts and their authors always take up lesson

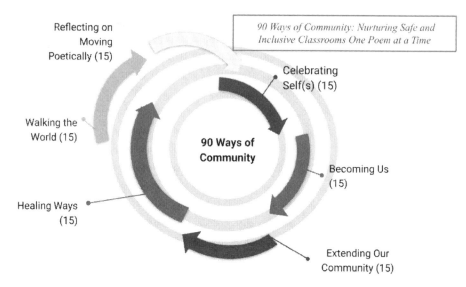

planning space in the English teacher department meetings. Teachers and students writing poetry daily, a brief warm-up ritual at the outset of class, becomes an intellectual practice that will expand their participation and understanding of these 'larger' English goals. But teachers and students writing poetry are often limited to National Poetry Month, if at all. We want English departments to talk about writing poetry as a valuable instructional and ontological (human) approach for a wide range of learning and being goals, so we offer clear instructions of easily modified lessons to keep conversations about writing poetry going all year long. We know that writing is recursive and being a writer is a lifelong journey.

To that end, we have organized this book around chapters that span a year of writing poetry that follows a year in the classroom that we have come to know and understand deeply: that when we first meet our students and they meet one another, the implicit questions on everyone's mind are who are these people, will they see me in a way that makes me feel good, and what is my place among them. And as we get to know one another, we can expand these questions to understand our community, the nation, the world, and our futures. We provide you with a variety of poetic practice lessons you can modify based on the specific needs of your classroom. The best use of this book is to familiarize yourself with the premise and the framework so you can actively modify and seek new ways to design meaningful connections with the other units of instruction you choose or are required to teach at your school.

- Chapter 1: Poetic Beginning or Getting Started
- Chapter 2: Celebrating Self(s)
- Chapter 3: Becoming Us
- Chapter 4: Welcoming Neighbors
- Chapter 5: Healing Ways
- Chapter 6: Walking the World
- Chapter 7: Reflecting on Moving Poetically
- Chapter 8: Concluding and Closure
- Appendix: Handouts and Resources

A Word about Structure

What we hope sets this book apart is that it is a book about poetic being. That is rather abstract; it does not mean we are walking around reciting poetry. Poetic being is a way of seeing, noticing, thinking, listening, and being with others that recognizes there are multiple meanings and interpretations and that we are, at heart, trying to do and be good with one another even if that means we notice unfairness or share pain. It is a way of remembering we are alongside others and that it is a privilege to witness another's life and to allow them to witness ours. We know that to work toward poetic being takes time and practice. And writing poetry together seems to get us pretty close to this idea.

We've made this book pretty easy to navigate, so if you want to focus on poetry about the world, you can go to the chapter with prompts about global poetic practice, for example without much trouble. To begin, though, some necessary organizational framing is helpful. Chapter 1 provides that theory we talked about and the concept of relational poetic practice along with some discussion of the state of writing instruction in US secondary classrooms right now. We also use this chapter to offer you a model for using all the prompts in the subsequent chapters. The role of this chapter is, more so, about setting up the routines in your classroom for success. We lay it out for the materials, practices, and even right down to the minute-by-minute steps you can use to do this work every day. We break down how you might grade this work to not undermine the poetic being with points and red pens. The other chapters begin with a Dear Teacher letter about the themes we explore and how the prompts can support students and you through the journey. We hope this offers you a rationale to help you and your students ease into the chapter's poetic practice and describe the broad and specific ways you might support students.

We sometimes reference poems and sources not in this book, and you can find most of them with a quick search on the World Wide Web. In other cases, we recommend a book of poems. It is up to you if you want to order a copy of the book for your poetic growth. You don't need the book to write a poem.

Most of our inspirations are free verse and topic-focused, but we want students to have choice as poets make all sorts of decisions in their craft, so we offer a table in the glossary with a variety of forms that students can use any day, for any prompt. They may be familiar with the form or need to explore it with a little research. We have a list of forms in a table that can be easily pasted into the notebook, so encourage students to reject or revise the poetry prompt any day to serve their purposes and preferences. For example, we have a prompt about researching a piece of art and offer a Mentor Poem that is free verse, but maybe the student wants or needs a form, so they could do a Lazy Sonnet.

Why 90 Prompts?

We know that there are about 180 days of school every year, and we know that that does not mean there are 180 days of instruction. With field days, field trips, assemblies, homecoming events, game days, fire drills, lockdown drills, holidays, cold days, snow days, and half days – well, you get the idea – we know that offering you 180 writing prompts will be too much, and you may feel defeated if you can't get through them all. For this reason, we offer 15 prompts for a time period that might correspond to different phases of the school year to intentionally nurture community and many ways of poetic thinking. Some sections may span a couple of months; for example "Celebrating Self(s)" could be from August through September and stretch into October. And "Becoming Us," might begin in October and stretch into November, and so on. In other words, we are trying to acknowledge that time and timing varies.

We'd also want you to feel like you have choices and can adapt as needed. We don't want you to feel pressure to do this every day or feel bad if you miss a day. Also, we recommend you use Friday as a reflection day, maybe an Open Mic day. See Chapter 2. Maybe this could be a day to revise a poem from earlier in the week or some workshopping time based on feedback.

Differentiation & Translanguaging

We include differentiation and translanguaging in our suggested lesson plan because we want you to attend to learning variances. We suggest ways the poetic routine can be inclusive and affirming-- even gentle.

We think the heat map, 1=18, and the forms chart that is included in Chapter 2 will go a long way in differentiating. Still, you will find that students need your explicit guidance and maybe permission to blend forms, draft in prose, skip prompts, draw, free write, or outright reject the prompt if needed. Use this as a diagnostic and formative assessment to adjust your routines for that student and ask them what they need.

Herrera and España (2022) offer important principles for teachers to consider when selecting Mentor Poems, themes, and languaging support in their classrooms. We want to encourage you to make clear that students can bring their entire linguistic repertoire to their poetic practice, writing in their home language or regional dialect as it is meaningful for them.

For teachers, it is important to self-reflect and unpack our language ideologies: What are my ideas around my language practices? What about my thoughts on students' language practices? How did those ideas evolve and how do they influence my teaching?

We also may have to do some unlearning of oppressive practices that have historically silenced or shamed (even stifled) our students' language choices and ways of writing. Whose language practices do I value or hold up as "right" or "correct"? Who decides what falls into these categories? What can I do to heal the harm so that students can feel safe in taking risks or using previously shamed writing?

Finally, show and celebrate languages and languaging as innovative and beautiful. What examples can you provide to show students various mentors and possibilities for their writing (and do so with joy)? How can you encourage students to use their entire range of linguistic resources from home, community, and histories to make meaning and connections?

We hope the poetry prompts offered here do that, but we recognize that your school community is yours and you know it best. Thus, please revise prompts and trade out poems for ones that show and lift up your students and communities.

The practical examples we offer in this chapter are a composite from practicing teachers and their students. We tried to make the sample lesson plan rather general in the hopes that the specific examples and ideas you and your students will surface will come from your particular context, place in the world, and the needs of your community. For instance, though a sample poem mentions a specific city, you might prompt students to think of their ranch or farm to find another poem topic for the day. Or if the Mentor Poem is relatable to a student who has a part-time job, it may seem unrelatable to a middle school student. Then again, it may not; many of Sarah's junior high students worked with their parents on weekends. This reminder or connection to the poem – this relationality – comes best when the teacher knows their students, and if you follow this book from day one, after a few weeks, you will know them (and they each other) quite well.

Let's start poem-ing – no, the foundations and framework chapter is next, but you can write a poem about that if you wish.

Oh, That's Right Copyright

The authors of the poems here own individual copyright and have agreed to share their poems in this book and online under the Creative Commons license CC BY-NC-SA: Attribution-NonCommercial-Share-Alike. This allows others to remix, adapt, and build upon the work non-commercially, as long as they credit the creator and license their new creations under the identical terms.

This book is an Open Educational Resource (OER). OER are educational materials that are freely accessible and openly licensed for anyone to use, adapt, and redistribute. They aim to reduce costs and improve access to education.

How OER Work Within Copyright

1. Licensing: Creators of OER use licenses to specify how others can use their work. The most common licenses are from Creative Commons (CC).

2. Creative Commons Licenses: The license for this book and the poems within is the following. CC BY-NC-SA: Attribution-NonCommercial-ShareAlike. Allows others to download, print, remix, adapt, and build upon the work non-commercially, as long as they credit the creator and license their new creations under the identical terms.

Benefits of Using OER

1. Cost Reduction: Freely accessible educational materials reduce the cost of educational resources for students.

2. Adaptability: Educators can adapt and customize OER to better suit their teaching needs and local contexts.

3. Collaboration: Facilitates collaboration and sharing among educators and institutions.

Ensuring Compliance

1. Attribution: Always give appropriate credit, provide a link to the license, and indicate if changes were made.

2. Understand License Terms: Be sure to understand and follow the terms of the specific Creative Commons license applied to the OER.

3. Respect Non-OER Content: Be cautious with incorporating non-OER content that may have stricter copyright protections.

By understanding and utilizing Creative Commons licenses, educators and content creators can share their work more freely and contribute to the growing body of OER, thereby enhancing educational access and equity.

Chapter 1: Poetic Beginning or Getting Started

In this chapter, we walk you through the daily practice of writing poetry with your students. After we discuss each step, there is a complete lesson that many teachers have piloted in their own classrooms with great success. If you follow this guide, you will have a successful poetic experience with students, but we also recommend that you modify the plan for your students' interests, needs, and ages. There are lots of ways you can adjust the poetic experiences to align with the units of instruction that you are already doing in your classroom or that your professional learning community (PLC) is working on. We'd love for your PLC to adopt this practice, but you can do it even if your colleagues are not ready. They will witness the benefits and join you in no time.

Okay, so you are ready to get started. We recommend that you begin every class with this poetic routine, but you may decide to try it one day a week or on certain days. Some teachers might call it Poetic Tuesdays, for example, and then add on additional days as you see the benefits. Still, we think the greatest benefits of poetry come from writing poetry every day. The poetic thinking (e.g., figurative, detailed, imaginative) nurtures a respect for language and the subject of the poetry. You will also see students developing a gentleness for themselves and their peers as they learn to share their craft, process, poetic lines, and creative takes on a variety of subjects and in a range of forms. So whether you do this daily or once a week, we recommend following the same routine so that students know what to expect and learn where they can make imaginative choices with words, form, and topics.

Setting Up the Notebook: Paper or Digital

We recommend students have a paper or digital notebook for their poetry. If you do this across the school year, their daily or weekly writing will become an important anthology of their learning and writerly development. This is your first decision, but you can also invite students to decide.

The paper notebook minimizes digital distraction and welcomes students to see and use their physical script rather than a mechanized font for typing. The paper tracks their scratches and drawings, part of the writing process and in-process revisions that are common to all writers. This is real and authentic. You may wish to keep these notebooks in the room so that students do not lose them, but some students will not trust them left behind and may want to write at home. Of course, students can have a school notebook and another notebook for home.

The digital notebook welcomes a different kind of experience. Sarah, for example, can type much faster than she can scribe, and she depends on a thesaurus when writing poetry. Being able to access another tab for words, synonyms, antonyms, and rhymes is helpful. Also, some of the prompts will invite you to try a poem generator (e.g., pantoum, a technical poem). Some poems ask students to do a little research like looking for a historic photograph or an art piece. This is an effective use of the internet. So, having a digital notebook allows for inquiry, digital poetry, and media-text writing.

However, Sarah found that the paper notebook offered a much-needed digital break for students. Students were also able to shift their writing positions in their desks or move to the floor or lean against a wall to curl up with their notebooks in ways they couldn't with their devices. And, they liked to draw, scratch, sketch, and add notes around their poems, which was easier to do with a pen or pencil.

If students needed their device to search a poem form, or use a thesaurus or rhyme generator, they still wrote in their notebook, so this minimized distractions of multiple tabs. Have you ever looked at your students' devices? Some have dozens of tabs open at once.

Day One

On the first day of the poetry workshop, you may want to dive right in with the first prompt, but we think you should spend a day setting up the routines and gathering some baseline data about how students think and feel about writing and themselves as a writer.

As we noted in Chapter 1, you and your students should decide if you want to use a paper or digital notebook for poetry writing, and we have offered our view on the affordances and limitations of both mediums. But, we do think you should commit to one, at least for a quarter at a time so that there is continuity and so you can have a holder to track the students' (and your) poetry.

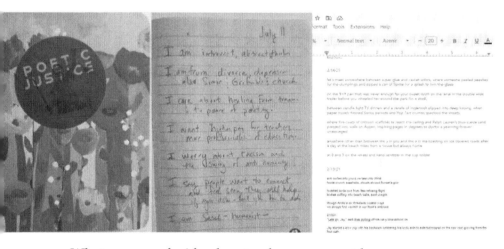

Whatever you decide, dear teacher, you must have your own notebook. Sarah starts a new notebook every semester and can be seen carrying it around at school. She begins every class holding a notebook and a pen, which is a signal to the students to do the same. It is part of the routine. During COVID-19, Sarah kept a paper notebook but also wanted to keep a digital notebook because all her students were remote, and she wanted to have access to their notebooks for periodic assessment. This was a tricky line to walk because the idea about the notebook space is that it is private. Just having the notebook in digital form means it can be shared and even passed around. We understand that a notebook can travel, too, but at least the student will know if the paper notebook is in someone else's hands. The digital notebook can be seen by the teacher at any time, so there is a privacy issue to consider.

Still, Sarah admits that the digital notebook was handy and that she could write on it through her device from anywhere. Either way, she easily located both notebooks for this chapter. See image.

Your students need to see your writing. They need to know that you are experiencing similar challenges and joys with the various prompts, and the collective act of writing poetry at the same time, in the same room, with one another shifts our understanding of what writing can do. The act of writing is, perhaps, more important than the products that emerge.

Once you have your notebook, you can help your students prepare their notebooks.

We suggest you skip the first couple of pages of the paper notebook because those inevitably fall out. Then tell them to reserve the first 4 pages for their table of contents. This way, students can track their poetry writing and writerly decisions.

Ask students to set up the first page of their table of contents. You and your students can choose the headings, which can vary quarter by quarter. For this example, we include the following headings: date, topic, form, craft moves, mode, and rating.

- **Date:** For the date, this will indicate the days you write poetry. Some days students will be absent. They can just skip that entry. You are doing so much writing, that they don't need to have a certain number for a grade. There is a lot of evidence in the notebook if you do decide to give a grade for the notebook.
- **Topic:** Some days the topic is embedded in the prompt. For example, the Genetic Cinquain is about family. Other days, the prompt is a form, and the topic is left up to the student. For example, the Skinny poem is a form, and the student can choose the topic. (See Heart Map.)
- **Form:** Like "topic" the form varies from day to day. So, again, with the Genetic Cinquain, the form is a cinquain.

For the prompt "Weddings and Recess," There is no suggested form or topic, so the student may write a free verse or select another form from their forms list (which you will paste into notebooks next.)

- **Craft Moves**: This column is here because some of the prompts offer or show specific craft moves such as interesting punctuation, alliteration, rhyming, no capital letters, simile, sensory language, etc. Students will gradually try new craft moves, so as much as you can, teacher, name the moves you notice in the Mentor Poems and talk about the craft moves you try. This is a way of teaching craft inductively, which can go a lot further than worksheets.

- **Mode**: Because most standards related to writing revolve around the modes of narrative, argument, and information, you can help students notice the ways they use these modes in their poetry. For example, a poem can tell the story of an important event (narrative). A poem can inform readers about nature or basketball or birds or any number of things, especially when the tone is quite observational. And if a poem is advocating for something or has a strong commentary or stance on an issue, the mode is likely argumentative.

- **Rating**: We found that tracing the emotional feelings around writing that day is helpful for students (and teachers who glance at the ratings) in recognizing patterns and preferences. For example, students may realize they prefer free verse--that some forms create discomfort or frustrations. They may also realize that they love a particular form, so on days when they are not feeling great, they may choose that form because it brings them joy or comfort.

Sidenote about grading: Most states have a standard for independent writing. For example, it may say something like this: *Students will write independently for short and extended periods. Students will vary their modes of expression to suit the audience and task.* This notebook is evidence of the "vary." Thus, each quarter, students can submit their notebooks with a reflection to demonstrate evidence of their awareness of mode of expression, audience, and task. (See Chapter 8.)

Date	Topic	Form	Craft Moves	Mode
9/10/23	Basketball	The Skinny	Repetition	Narrative
9/13/23	Genetics	Cinquain	Shape	Informational
9/20/23	Swimming	Free	Alliteration	Argument

Heart Map: "I don't know what to write about."

Because students must make decisions about a topic, we encourage you to spend the first day (or someday in the first week) building a resource of topics for students. We have certainly heard our students say, "But I don't have anything to write about." And instead of spending time every day giving suggestions or inviting students to think about how the Mentor Poem is exploring a topic that could inspire the student's writing, we recommend borrowing from Georgia Heard's work in *Awakening the Heart* (1999). Nancie Atwell has a similar brainstorming activity called "Writing Territories." You can find many lessons on how to conduct this brainstorming activity on the internet. Sarah has used the Heart Map every year with her students from seventh-grade classrooms to doctoral seminars. Here are several reasons:

- The heart serves as a metaphor for what all writers know; to write is to delve into what matters to us...to tell the truth, to question, and to speak what many

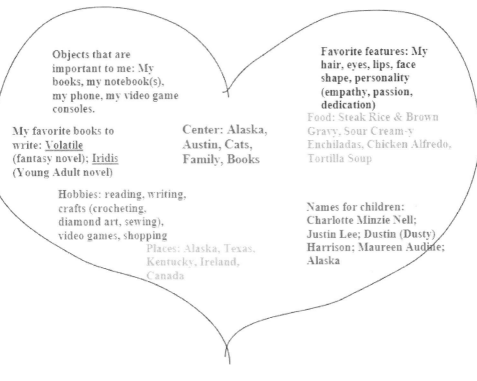

Objects that are important to me: My books, my notebook(s), my phone, my video game consoles.

My favorite books to write: Volatile (fantasy novel); Iridis (Young Adult novel)

Hobbies: reading, writing, crafts (crocheting, diamond art, sewing), video games, shopping

Center: Alaska, Austin, Cats, Family, Books

Places: Alaska, Texas, Kentucky, Ireland, Canada

Favorite features: My hair, eyes, lips, face shape, personality (empathy, passion, dedication)

Food: Steak Rice & Brown Gravy, Sour Cream-y Enchiladas, Chicken Alfredo, Tortilla Soup

Names for children: Charlotte Minzie Nell; Justin Lee; Dustin (Dusty) Harrison; Maureen Audine; Alaska

people only keep inside.
- The visual, concrete drawing holds concrete and abstract inspirations: "Because writing is contained within a visual shape of a heart, it tends to be less abstract and becomes a kind of visual and emotional blueprint for writers to map people, memories, and experiences significant to them."
- The heart metaphor and the brainstorming on the page is a scaffold that supports the writer emotionally and academically in the spirit of play, creativity, and

exploration. This process generates multiple ideas to open up a topic.

- The process of creating a heart map individually and collectively in the shared creative space energizes the classroom, and that energy is reignited every time the teacher or peer says, "You don't know what to write about today? Check your heart map." It is filled with things the writer cares about.

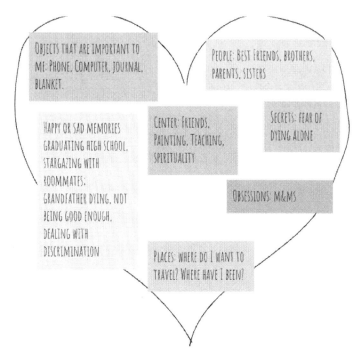

- Building on the previous point (and others) the heart is the center of your writing community (classroom). After you create the heart map, students share them, and this sparks even more ideas while nurturing trust and connection for our similarities and our differences. We all have stories, expertise, and knowledge that can teach others. Students' writing can *be* the curriculum.

To begin, you will invite students to open their notebook to the first page of their notebook (after the Table of Contents). They can draw a heart or any other object of importance to them. This can be landscape or portrait. One page or two pages. And, it can be done using the drawing feature of a Google Doc or slide. (See many videos here: https://www.georgiaheard.com/heart-maps)

Some questions to help you get started with heart mapping:
- What memories have you stored in your heart (they don't have to be BIG or exciting memories. For example, the smell of molasses cookies baking in the oven at my grandmother's house is an important memory to me because it was something she would always do.)
- What people have been important to you – and why?
- What are some experiences or events that you will never forget?
- What happy or sad memories do you have?
- What secrets do you keep in your heart?
- What things or objects are important to you -- for example, a tree in your backyard or a stuffed animal, etc.?
- What's at the center of your heart – you might want to place the most important people, memories, and experiences in the center?
- Ask yourself if you want to keep some things inside your heart and less important things on the outside of your heart.
- Do you want to draw more than one heart – good and bad; happy and sad; secret and open – and include different things inside each heart?
- Do different colors represent different emotions, events, and relationships?

When you do this activity with your students, it is so important for you, the teacher, to do this, too, so that students can engage with you and see the sorts of topics and thinking about the topics that elicit writing possibilities for you.

A tip that we found, with the advice of Georgia Heard, is that writing down words like "travel" or "vacation" doesn't do much to get at the specifics that can illuminate a poetic representation of that experience. As you model this, then, try for specific words or phrases that inspire such as "dead bee in funnel cake--Destin, FL vacation" or "one-pound package of Twizzlers" rather than "candy."

The example heart maps shared in this chapter are from two of Sarah's students who created heart maps in their digital notebooks. You can see the pattern of guidance that Sarah used when modeling the process for students. And you can see how some of the topics that made it onto the map are general while others are specific.

1. The center is for people, places, things, and memories at the center of our hearts -- most important.
2. In the margins are ideas such as
   - favorites: parts of ourselves, things, people, places, foods, memories
   - objects of importance
   - media: books, shows, music, apps, formative video games
   - places that bring you comfort/discomfort or joy/sadness
   - obsessions or hobbies
   - secrets

Topics: "But *how* do I actually write about these things?"

Another idea for generating topics to write about in various modes is an activity from Kelly Gallager, called 1 to 18. Students can take one topic from their heart map and then explore it in 18 ways using various text structures of informational and argumentative writing.

The heart map will work for many students, but you will still have students who cannot come up with an angle, lens, or way into one of their ideas. For example, Sarah had students who were great fútbol players and loved everything fútbol (or soccer). Still, students didn't understand or believe that writing was a place for them to share their expertise or to spend time thinking about something they loved --- while they were at school.

1 Topic+18 Topics - NYC	
Purpose	Possible Writing Topics
Express and Reflect *feel/lessons*	• How I came to live in New York (& what it took to get there) • What I learned about myself from living there
Inform and Explain *Tell something about your topic* *that the reader might not know*	• The weird microcosm of any given subway car • How to avoid eye contact with strangers so they don't try to get anything out of you • How I accidentally got my most favorite coffee job ever
Evaluate and Judge *Worth & value, good/bad,* *best/worst*	• Best parts about NYC that I still wax nostalgic over • Worst parts about living in New York that nobody ever tells you •
Inquire and Explore *Wrestle with a question*	• Did NYC make me a better or a worse person? • Did it permanently change my personal growth trajectory or would I have wound up in the same place without NYC? • Do I regret leaving? • Why is NYC seen as the best place for writers?
Analyze and Interpret *the why behind*	• Why did I idolize NYC? • Why do we need more and wider experiences to grow as writers?
Take a Stand/Propose a Solution *Problems, injustice, should be,* *ought to be*	• Getting out of your comfort zone by moving somewhere new forces you to grow as a person, which can impact your writing

We share an example here from a student who moved from New York City to Chicago; they had so much knowledge of their home (real insider details) that they could share with our class in poetry, and this also assuaged the student's homesickness when they chose to write about New York City from time to time.

Forms Chart (Appendix)

Another step in setting up the notebook is to paste in the forms chart. You and your students should paste this onto a page in the back. Writers make choices. We want students to get used to making choices to nurture their writerly agency and embrace autonomy rather than be paralyzed by decisions. With most prompts, students will be choosing the topic, form, or both, so we want students (and you) to have a quick reference sheet for options. Many of these forms are familiar to students and can be easily applied during the time frame you provide, but others will require some inquiry, some research. Welcome this. If a student has an idea for the poem but wants to try a new form, you can print out instructions for them, but they can also do a quick search to read about it. Maybe they don't get their poem written that day, but they will be ready for the next day with their new form.

In our chart of poem forms, we want to be clear that this is a simplistic way of sorting the forms so that students can make decisions about complexity and structure. We hope that in seeing this list that students may, in fact, invent new forms and begin to write their own prompts for the poetic experiences you have. Maybe you will forgo this book at some point because you have a room full of poets that have better ideas -- or at least more relevant and personal to your class community.

When a poet writes, they make all sorts of decisions to help them make or find meaning, and we want students to recognize all of this as craft and all as opportunities for students to draw on poetic features to tell their stories, and share their observations of the world. We recommend the book *Poetic Forms: 100 Poetic Forms, Definitions, and Examples for Poets* by Robert Lee Brewer for your classroom.

- **Form:** We define poetic form as a combination of poetic features like stanzas, lines, meter, syllables per line, topic, rhyme scheme, and any patterns of repetition of words, lines, rhythms and such.
- **Stanza:** A stanza is a group of lines forming a basic structure or unit in a poem.
- **Lines:** Lines can refer to the number of lines in the entire poem or in a stanza; students may also use lines or stanzas to describe **enjambment**, the continuation of a sentence without a pause beyond the end of a line.
- **Meter/Syllables**: A meter is a pattern of beats, and syllables tend to be part of that pattern but are not always. Students can consider both, but we use this column to account for the counting pattern of a poem, if there is one. Some poems do not have a required syllable count per line but prefer the number of syllables per line to be consistent throughout. This is kind of like

repetition because the repeated pattern of the syllabus creates a musical rhythm in the poem.

- **Typical Topic**: Some poems tend to be for contemplating a specific topic. For example, the original haiku considers nature. Other forms do not have a specific topic but may have a tone such as humorous (limerick) or formal (ode).
- **Rhyme Scheme:** A pattern of sound between words or at the end of words, especially when repeated within or at the end of lines of poetry -- this is the rhyme scheme. Some poems decidedly do not rhyme, like haiku, but others depend on it, such as the sonnet.
- **Pattern of Repetition:** Rhyme is the repetition of sound, and there is the repetition of words, lines, phrases, or some pattern of emphasis even if the exact sequence is not repeated. For example, the Skinny poem repeats the same word in lines 2, 6, and 10. And, lines 1 and 11 repeat a similar sentence -- same words but rearranged for different meanings. There are also repeated images.

Throughout this book, we focus on themes of poetry and invite students (and you) to make decisions about the topic and form. We do this because we don't want writing poetry to be too didactic or strict. Also, some forms of poetry are quite complex and take time to write. Poems with strict rhyme schemes or patterns tend to require additional resources like a thesaurus (Sarah always writes poetry with a thesaurus tab open) or a rhymes-with-type website. We encourage you to carve time for students to explore various forms as time allows. If we explicitly suggest a form for one of the prompts included in the book, we indicate that in the Forms Table.

A Walk Through a Poetic Experience (10-ish Minutes)

Lesson planning is really important because the plan helps you intentionally design learning experiences that have a clear focus, scaffold learning, give students opportunities for guided practice and collaboration, and hold onto the reason why we even read and write. We recommend that you use the plan that follows in the first weeks of these poetic experiences so that you are using the scaffolds we have found to be helpful and humanizing.

If you skip this and use past structures like bell ringers that direct students to comply with the standard activity without framing or scaffolding or engagement with relational ways of writing, the poetic benefits could be lost.

And, one more thing, our teacher-poet-friend Allison Berryhill from Iowa has great advice for us as we write with students: "Here is my next hint for sustaining your momentum: Be kind to yourself. Look at your poem [and your students'] as if it had been written by your son, or your mother, or someone you love. See the good in it. Glance past its weaknesses. Acknowledge that each poem is a tender thing, trying to say something, trying to be heard."

Below is a mini-lesson plan for the first 10-ish minutes of class that includes typical features like the following: standard, materials, essential questions, introducing the prompt, guided thinking, independent practice, and closing transition to your main lesson of the day. Next, we describe the various features of the poetic mini-lesson and then have a template that you can use with almost every prompt.

We recommend you create a slide deck that you use and reuse each day so that students know and feel the routine.

Procedure for Launching the Class with Writing Poetry

In this section, we offer a suggested lesson plan and a sample lesson to walk you through, start-to-finish, how to start your class with a mentor poem, invite writing, and nurture sharing in about ten minutes.

1. Standard. Each poetry prompt offers an opportunity to uncover several reading and writing standards. And every poetic experience also engages speaking and listening. Thus, all the prompts here meet multiple standards. Still, you may be working on something specific in your unit of instruction.

Perhaps you are doing a research unit, so you might want students to integrate some inquiry into their writing. You may want students to focus on figurative language, so that might be a goal in the writing.

2. Materials to Gather. The prompt has all the materials you need for poetic routines, but you may want to create a slide deck or use a scanner to project the details of the prompt for students. In each prompt, we offer you a Mentor Poem to inspire the learners' topic, poetic form, and language choices. We also select Mentor Poems that offer students inclusive-affirming and diverse representations of social identities (e.g., gender, race, culture, language, ability). Students love to see pictures of poets, especially if the poet is from their own culture or background and, honestly, young-ish. We recommend you introduce students to living poets, so that students see themselves as living poets, too. Typically, these are the materials you will need:

1. Student notebooks (paper or digital);
2. Projector with a copy of the poem and/or copies of poems to tape into notebooks;
3. Mentor Poem notes; and
4. Author image/bio if relevant and accessible.

3. Essential Question for Focus. The point of this is to help students think about the poem's meaning. Too often, poetry is taught as something to decode or interpret part-by-part. But poems are meant to be read for their wholeness, for the way all the parts work together to do something or say something. And, the truth is that many times the poet couldn't tell you exactly what the poem means. The meaning was in the making of the poem, and now the poem lives in the space between the text and the reader. The reader brings new meaning to the poem. Thus, an essential question helps us think about why we read and write poetry. What poetry does for us that other forms don't? These can be your essential questions. However, you may have others related to your unit of instruction. You may be studying a historical period like the Jim Crow era, so you might want to swap out our Mentor Poem for another, and your question might be how poets represent the injustice of that time or how we still experience elements of Jim Crow today.

4. Inspiration Script. The example that follows includes a script of what to say when you introduce a poem. This is not meant to be patronizing. We intend to give you a sense of how this looks live, in action. Try it out. Make your script. Do away with the script after you find your own voice and way of being with this process.

> The bell rings. I introduce the prompt.

> "Today we are thinking about what experiences from our past shape who you are today. You may be thinking of the day you got a puppy or maybe something more memorable like the loss of a loved one. The way we are in those moments sheds light into who we are, so today we will write a few lines inspired by the amazing Clint Smith's 'Something You Should Know.'"

5. Process. After offering some options to the students, you may be tempted to put them to writing, but this is a key step to uncovering the poetic moves that students may want to imitate or disrupt in their own writing. Each poem offers multiple moves you can notice, but just focus on a couple. In this sample lesson, we highlight the structure of the poem that begins a list, and then we note the vivid details like the verb "tamped the espresso." We also note the closing and how the poet offers what Nancie Atwell calls the "so what." This draws students' attention to the craft of the poem so they can be intentional in their writing over time.

6. Students Write. In this part, students write. We like the writing guideline of "no walk, no talk" to nurture safe writing spaces. Students know not to move around the room or talk to a peer. Be sure sharpened pencils and pens are nearby so students don't have to seek a utensil just as they are starting to write. Also, we want students to keep writing the entire time -- again, so they don't distract others. Tell students they can change the topic, draw, or return to another prompt, but they should keep going for whatever time you decide. We think this timing depends on your class culture and the age of students -- and also the prompt-- but 5 to 10 minutes is good. We also want you to write, too, but only for the first couple of minutes. This daily writing time is also assessment time. Give it a couple of minutes for students to start, and then move around the room. This is where differentiation comes in.

7. Differentiation. If you notice a student has not yet begun to write, kneel down and ask the student how things are going. Sometimes they are thinking or planning. Sometimes they are stuck. Ways to support them might be to talk through the first couple of lines and then ask them to write that down. You might write the first couple lines together and then ask them what might come next. You can also suggest drawing and then writing words to describe the picture. Students may want to write in prose first -- paragraph-- and then later shift it to a poem. Any of these options are great, but it is always best to ask a student how you can help first.

8. Translanguaging. We want students to draw on their entire language repertoire. Translanguaging is much more fluid than separation of languages. It is the way students think, write, speak, and the way teachers teach. It is a pedagogical approach that may include a text in English but conversations, prompts, notes, and responses are in other languages. We want students to see poems in multiple languages and to encourage multilingual writing -- in our texts, classroom walls, notebooks, and conversations around the room. Encourage students to use language software, have bilingual glossaries, and pair students strategically for sharing.

9. Sharing for Belonging. The sharing part is essential for nurturing safe spaces. We cannot declare safety as it is up to everyone in the room. And sharing our writing can be scary as it requires some vulnerability to show quick drafts of our writing, but this is part of the culture shift in your classroom. You can mix up the sharing depending on time. Some days, students may share with an elbow partner and not comment; other days, there may be a compliment using the 3-Ways Protocol. We like to have a relational way of deciding who shares first such as "whoever has longer hair" shares first. That person reads -- does not summarize, but reads-- their poem. The other person responds with a sentence of ethos, pathos, or logos. They switch. On other days, we have students stand and find a new partner whom they have yet to talk to for sharing. This promotes a culture of sharing and relationships in the classroom, and students benefit from moving around the room and reading while standing. Sharing is practice in speaking and listening. The listener may struggle at the beginning of the year, but their ear does develop for recognizing craft moves and attending to poetic messages. Use the response guide by projecting it on the screen as students share. Walk around the room to gently redirect them to offer writerly responses or their meaning-making process. Writers benefit from a window into

Complimenting writers: Be sure to use their names in your response to them. Below are three perspectives you might consider when crafting your compliments:

From the heart (pathos)	From the mind (logos)	From the writer in me (ethos)
Respond by sharing a memory that surfaced for you. Did you have a similar experience? Did this remind you of something from your life?	What did the writer say that you liked, learned from, never considered before this moment? Did you like the way the writer pointed out (something)?	What did you like about how it was written? Sound: rhyme, repeating lines, alliteration. Pace: short phrases, long phrases, one word. Imagery: a verb, image, pun, simile, metaphor, sensory detail (color, texture of objects).
• I can relate to the phrase "..." because.... • When you wrote "...," I felt/was reminded ...because... • Your words "..." really moved me/resonated with me because...	• The phrase "..." got me thinking about...because... • Until I read/heard your words "...," I had not considered...in this way. Now I see... • I see or understand ...in a new way after reading ...because... • I think the heart of this piece is in the line "..." because	• I noticed you used the technique of ...in the phrase/stanza...: it's effect is... • A vivid word is... because... • A clever line is ...because... • Your use of ... gives the effect...

Adapted from Donovan, S.J. (2015). 3 perspectives improve peer-to-peer response. *Middle Web.* https://www.middleweb.com/24247/3-perspectives-can-improve-peer-to-peer-response/

the readers' experience more than critique or suggestions. Sharing time is only for compliments of craft. See "peer conferring" for more on this.

10. Full-Circle Closing or Transition. Some days you will want to extend the sharing because so many great writerly conversations are happening, but eventually, you will need to transition to the day's lesson, so develop your own process for this or just say: *Okay, now add your writing to your table of contents and then let's turn to [whatever you have next on your agenda].* Students can turn to their table of contents and write their entry for the day. This will be useful for midterm and end-of-semester grading when you invite students to do some reflection, goal setting, and portfolio work for that independent writing standard. We recommend that you also use this time to make some connection between the mentor poem or things you heard the students talking about in their sharing that can emphasize the ideas in your unit. For example, you may point out the point of view, vivid and figurative language, conflict, setting, theme, mood, and/or tone that fits with your unit.

11. Additional Resources. Finally, in the sample lesson below, we connect you to the original resource of the poem prompt with additional mentor texts and variations. Here there are models of reader-response, too, that may help you and students see that the kind of feedback most helpful for writers is a window into the reader's experience. We encourage you to gather additional resources that are relevant to your curriculum, course, grade level, and community needs. For example, if you are teaching AP Literature, you might explicitly draw connections between the "Masks We Wear" prompt in Chapter 3 with Paul Laurence Dunbar's poem "We Wear the Mask." Of course, we can't include the poem here due to copyright, but you likely have it in your textbook.

Sample Lesson: Something You Should Know

Steps	Procedure	Teacher Tip
1. Standard	Write informative texts to examine a topic and convey ideas, concepts, and information through the selection, and organization of relevant content.	Not all informational writing needs to be in prose. It can be in poetry, too.
2. Materials to Gather	1. Student notebooks 2. Projector with a copy of the poem and/or copies of poems to tape into notebooks 3. Mentor Poem: Smith, C. (n.d.). Something you should know. *The American Poetry Review, 45*(6). https://aprweb.org/poems/something-you-should-know	If you do this daily, students do well with a paper notebook to hold all their writing. They love to tape or paste poems & resources into their notebook; this creates ownership.
3. Essential Question for Focus	What experiences from our past help shape who we are today?	This will vary depending on your scope & sequence.
4. Inspiration Script 3 minutes	The essential question and Mentor Poem should be projected on the board before students come in with a note to take out their notebooks or to ready their Chromebooks to write. The bell rings. *Today we are thinking about what experiences from our past shape who you are today. You may be thinking of the day you got a puppy or maybe something more memorable like the loss of a loved one. The way we are in those moments sheds light into who we are, so today we will write a few lines inspired by the amazing Clint Smith's "Something You Should Know."* Option A: Project Clint Smith's poem on the screen and/or show a picture of Clint Smith. Read his poem. There may be copyright issues.	Canva or Slides offer a variety of ways to format the poem and prompt on one slide. Smith's and his poems are fantastic; it's really important for students to see contemporary, living male poets.

Option B. California teacher and instructional coach Emily Yamasaki wrote this poem which is an Open Education Resource, meaning you can print and share freely:

So that you can see teachers writing poetry, we share Emily's poem to inspire you.

Something You Should Know

is that when I was young, I once worked as a Kelly's Coffee barista.
I greeted patrons
of all ages, baked blueberry scones, and
of course, made caffeinated beverages.
I tamped the espresso neat
and tidy, like a hockey puck, into the wand
leaving zero trace of crumb on the edges.
Espresso grind is notoriously messy,
Which only gave me more resolve to
meticulously pack it, manage it, control it.
Perhaps that i when I became
obsessed with having a spot for everything.
Perhaps that is why, even now,
when I get the desperate urge to
leave a crumb,
I'm afraid so
I sweep them all neatly away.

5. Process

So we learn something about Emily from her poem. Yes, she worked in a coffee shop, but we can understand that she is also "obsessed" with neatness.

Notice the structure here:
  1) *Topic: "I once worked as a Kelly's Coffee barista." So what have students done: a chore on the farm, babysitting a sibling, making dinner, taking piano lessons, and loving Pokemon.*
  2) *Select details: Then there are vivid details (e.g., baked blueberry scones, tamped the espresso).*
  3) *Convey an idea: And then there is a third part, she tells what she learned from this – the so what beyond coffee. We learn about Emily's neatness.*

Where are some places you used to live, jobs you used to do, chores you used to have, hobbies you used to love/hate? Tell us something we should know about you.

Turn to your neighbor and say what you might write about today. Great. I heard some ideas.

This noticing or think-aloud with the students is the teaching. You may ask students to point out what they notice in how this poem is organized or how they might use this poem as inspiration for their own.

6. Students Write

Okay, so let's give ourselves about five minutes to see where the poem takes us today. If you get stuck, you can try a list or reject the prompt and write about whatever is in your heart and mind today.

When we write, the way we nurture a safe and supportive space is no walk, no talk.

Look around the room to be sure people have pencils sharpened.

I may move around to support you, but I will do my best not to distract you.

Set a timer.

Teacher, in your notebook, write the poem. Even if you've done it before, write about another topic so that you can practice the feeling of starting from a blank page. Notice where you went for ideas. Do you have a list of ideas somewhere in your notebook? Did you think back to a time or place in your life? Great. These ideas will help your student because about 2 minutes have passed, and now you need to take a lap around the room.

While they write, you are looking to be sure the notebooks are open, that students have a pen or pencil, that they are writing or drawing to sketch ideas. If a student is stuck, kneel down and ask them how you can help. They likely need to talk through things: past hobbies, past awards, places they've lived, chores they did. Ask for details. Then, show them the Mentor Poem and invite them to imitate the structure.

Always give students options in the prompt to select the topic, select the form, and/or reject both and write what they need that day. Students thrive on choice, agency, autonomy.

It is important to set this expectation of the writer's space. Typically, students will think for the first minute or so, then around minute 4 they will get into it. If you see everyone is engaged and you have time, extend the timer a few more minutes.

7. Differentiation

For students who struggle to come up with ideas, you will want to start the writing process. Give them 2 minutes, and then confer with the student by asking them these questions again. You may write the first line with them, then ask for a few details. To verbally talk through the poem will help them rehearse their writing.

8. Translanguaging	Students should always have the option to draw on their home languages to write in all or in part. If you see students doing this, celebrate it.	
9. Sharing for Belonging	Depending on time, you may have students do any of the following with an elbow partner: Quick: Tell your partner what you wrote about today. Brief: Exchange a favorite line you wrote today with a neighbor. Longer: Have one person read their poem while the other listens and then responds as a human, reader, or writer. Listen in as students share. Ask a few people to share, with consent from their partner, what they noticed in a neighbor's poem. This is part of creating a community of shared experiences and surfacing what makes good writing. See the 3-ways of responding chart.	Model the longer version with a student. Ask them to read their poem to you and then model how to use the sentence stems. Then, and this is important, they must be able to reciprocate and practice listening to you. Read your poem and invite them to respond to you. Ask a student to share what they said to their partner before you bring it to the whole group.
10. Full-Circle Closing or Transition to the next lesson	*Okay, now add your writing to your table of contents, and then let's turn to [whatever you have next on your agenda].* OR *Let's consider how this poem helps us answer our essential question….and remember the way… (skill, e.g., details make a concept come alive in informational writing).*	Have the students create a table of contents in their notebook – about 4 pages. They can write the date, the poem topic, and if the

Date	Topic	Type of Poem	Emoji
9/7	Things I love	List poem	☐
9/8	Something you should know	free verse	☐

poem was a free verse or another form. The emoji or other symbol will help them think about how they felt when writing. They can come up with their key for the symbols they use.

Note: You can "grade" the notebook at midterm and final each quarter by adding a reflection component to the table of contents. (See final chapter.)

11. Additional Resources   See Ethical ELA for the original post and many examples of teachers writing with this prompt. You can see a wide range of things you should know about teachers, and in knowing these experiences – wide and varied– we all feel seen. https://www.ethicalela.com/something-you-should-know /

Sharing for Belonging Extended: Friday Open Mic

We love this quote from our teacher-poet-friend, Allison Berryhill, who said this about sharing poetry with others: "Prepare for all the feels as you read others' poems and the responses to your own! "

Start with the Sign-Up

To prepare for the open mic, every student signs up to read one Friday. This is their commitment to read one poem for our community.

I explained at the beginning of the school year that this is essential to building a safe community of writers where we can contribute and benefit from the contributions of nearly thirty writers (our class). It is about the reciprocal nature of embodying and appreciating one another's willingness to be vulnerable. It is about recognizing that writers need readers and readers need writers. It is about valuing all the voices and authority of all the voices in our classroom.

In addition to signing up to share, I ask for two volunteers to be MCs or to host the open mic. Their job is to review the speaking and listening goals, to introduce the writers, and to facilitate the compliments. See the form Sarah uses to create our Friday calendar for open mic.

Open-Mic Calendar

	Monday	Tuesday	Wednesday	Thursday	Friday
1					1_____ 2_____ 3_____ 4_____ MC1_____ MC2_____
2					1_____ 2_____ 3_____ 4_____ MC1_____ MC2_____
3					1_____ 2_____ 3_____ 4_____ MC1_____ MC2_____
4					1_____ 2_____ 3_____ 4_____ MC1_____ MC2_____
5					1_____ 2_____ 3_____ 4_____ MC1_____ MC2_____
6					1_____ 2_____ 3_____ 4_____ MC1_____ MC2_____
7					1_____ 2_____ 3_____ 4_____ MC1_____ MC2_____
8					1_____ 2_____ 3_____ 4_____ MC1_____ MC2_____
9					Portfolio of presentations, reflection of favorite moments and growth in writers

Trust the MCs

The very first time, you will need to support the MCs, but after that, they will know what to do. The MCs have a few jobs. First, the day before the open mic, the two MCs check in with the four writers who will share on Friday. I ask the MCs to take the writers into the hallway or corner of the room and do a quick read-through with the writers. This is just to make sure the writers know they are sharing and have had at least one practice read.

Your Name _____ Celebrations for Quarter _____ Period _____

Something to celebrate about the author's writing!

- o **Jargon:** fancy words and words specific to the subject/topic (shows expertise/knowledge)
- o **Figurative language:** simile, metaphor, allusion, personification, hyperbole, anaphora, alliteration, assonance, consonance, oxymoron, anthropomorphism, apostrophe
- o **Sensory language:** smell, sound, taste, touch, sight -colors, shapes, textures, movement -- the setting/place comes alive, can imagine characters
- o **Logos:** facts, details, examples, research, reasoning, explanations, logic
- o **Pathos:** brave, vulnerable, insightful, emotional, powerful phrases, ideas
- o **Innovative:** unexpected lead, twist, ending, non cliche, inserting an epistle, poem, mixing genre forms, conclusion was fresh (something we haven't heard)
- o **Transitions:** subordinating conjunctions (when, while, after, before) show time/place/idea changes; conjunctive adverbs (thus, however, therefore, on one hand, on the other hand)
- o **Syntax:** starting with gerund, infinitive, subordinating conjunction, asyndeton, anaphora, parentheticals, appositives, parallelism

Name	Feature to Celebrate	Text Evidence	Check if you complimented the author. →	
1. Sarah	Sensory language -- smell	"rotting stench of a fish left in the garbage for days"		❑
2.				❑
3.				❑
4.				❑
5.				❑
6.				❑
7.				❑
8.				❑
9.				❑
10.				❑
11.				❑
12.				❑
13.				❑

On the day of the open mic, the MCs take the class through VEEPPP (see Appendix). This is our acronym for presentations: V (volume), have enough volume so that everyone in the room can hear your beautiful words; E (eye contact), take glances at the audience after dramatic dialogue or startling facts to acknowledge your audience and to witness their reaction to your craft; E (expression), match your vocal tone to your content with emotion, energy, interpretation so that the audience hears it how you wrote it; P (pace), match the pace with your content so that you slow down with difficult or complex ideas, allow us a breath to process a clever line or sensitive phrase; and P (professionalism), have a strong stance and focus as you read and afterward accept the applause, let it wash over you to give the audience a chance to show their appreciation.

During open mic, the hosts alternate introducing the next speaker and helping the speaker set up their Chromebook to record the presentation. The recordings, over time, become artifacts of their growth as readers and writers.

VEEPP	Public Speaking
Volume	We can hear you in the back of the room. You may make your voice louder or softer in certain parts to emphasize something, show passion/emotion, or make the audience lean in, but it is related to content. Your volume does not distract from your message.
Eye Contact	We can see your eyes at different points of the performance to show you are trying to connect with us – your audience. You can hold eye contact with 3 angles of the room, so you are showing you know your content well.
Expression	The way you say the words and phrases shows you are interpreting the mood and content to communicate to the audience. You may change your expression in different parts as the mood shifts or ideas become more serious or light-hearted.
Pace	You stay within the time allowed. You perform with a pace that matches the content and mood; it is slow enough for us to hear and process the words and fast enough for us to feel the rhythm. You may slow down to emphasize certain parts or to let an important idea really resonate with the audience.
Pronunciation	You practiced and know the words you've written, especially technical ones. The audience is not distracted by phrasing or unclear pronunciation.
Professionalism	You prepared for the performance. You stand strong (no swaying), say "thank you" at the end to signal closure, stay for a moment to accept the applause, and your demeanor treats the topic and audience with respect.

Figure 1 You can see the writer-presenter is in blue at the music stand. The boy sitting at the table in front of him is holding the writer's Chromebook to be sure it is documenting his reading. The rest of the students are listening, but you might be able to se

The Writer-Readers

The writer knows well in advance the date they will share, but we write on the board each week who the writers and MCs are, and throughout the week, the students are writing and chatting about who will share what with intention. As we are in the second quarter, the students know the routine and are thinking weeks in advance about what they want to share, but many find themselves excited about a new piece from that week's quick-writes and spend the night before open mic revising for the class.

The students hear what works well with the audience. They get a sense of what ideas engage the audience. They want to take a risk with the plot or try more description or dialogue because they noticed it was pleasing to them as an audience member. The writers in the room are shaping one another's craft in ways that defy measurement. It is organic.

Ask the writers to set a goal for their reading. Some need to do more with expression. Some need to learn the joy of swimming in the applause of the audience because they are so relieved to be done, they tend to rush away. As mentioned above, the day before the open mic, students practice attending to their goals.

On the day of their reading, students set up their Chromebook with Screencastify (an extension on Chrome) and cue up the webcam. An MC helps them set up the recording so that they can focus on the reading: "Hello, my name is (name), and today I will be sharing a (narrative, argument, informational piece, poem) about (topic)."

After that, they just read. And when they are finished. The audience waits for a "thank you" before applauding. (There is nothing worse than planning a dramatic pause only for the audience to start clapping. Awkward.) The writer then waits for the applause to wash over and through them, hopefully feeling a sense of satisfaction.

Students keep the recording of their reading in their Google Drive until the last week of the quarter when they watch-listen to it and reflect on the experience from this quarter. Then, they watch-listen to their recording from the previous quarter to reflect on their growth.

The Audience's Role

If four students are sharing and two students are hosting, then the rest of the students are listening. They are the audience members whose role is to enjoy the writing, support the writer, and notice examples of "good" writing. I give students a "listening sheet" for them to document their notes. This is also practice in identifying moves in writing and citing text evidence. See the Listening Sheet filled-out picture.

However, perhaps more important than listening and noticing is the applause. We practice making sure all pencils are down after the "thank you" from the writer-presenter so that all hands are free to clap and show appreciation for their classmate's writing and willingness to be vulnerable.

The Teacher's Role in Sarah's Experiences

I sit among the students during the open mic. I have my laptop open, and I take notes about the writer's craft and speaking skills. I write a personal note to the writer with celebrations of their writing and speaking. I tell them what I enjoyed, what I noticed, and what I suggest for next time, which is typically this: "Put a mark in the margin of your writing to remind yourself to look up at your audience. Make sure we are with you. See the joy in their eyes after you read a beautiful line or get to the plot twist. You don't want to miss out on their reactions."

I move around a bit to check in with the audience members to hear what they are whispering about (which is always something good about the writing) and, for some, I remind them to take a few notes so that they can participate in celebrations in the end. I used to share my writing, too, but I have found that it is best just to be on the fringes as much as possible so that the writing community can bond without my physical and vocal intrusions.

Compliments

This is the final part of the class. Celebrations are essential for our community building. The space has to be safe if everyone is going to have a positive experience sharing their writing and if everyone is going to *want* to offer their writing to the class. You may not believe me when I say that everyone shares and everyone really does enjoy this experience. It is true. Everyone feels safe, and I think it is because of the celebrations.

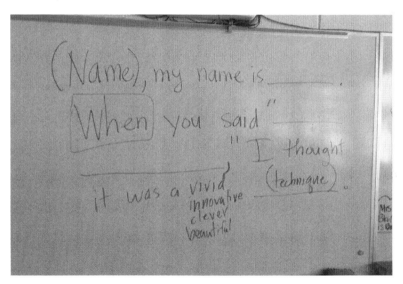

Here is how our MCs set up the celebrations:

"Okay, thank you, writers," says one MC.
After the applause subsides, he continues,
"Now for compliments. Remember to look at
the person you are celebrating and offer a
very specific compliment about the writing.
Try to use the complex sentence stem that
we are writing on the board."

This is what he writes on the board.

> "Yeah, so get ready now, maybe practice in
> your mind what you will say because we are
> all going to give compliments. And oh,
> writers," the other MC adds on, "make sure
> you also look at the person complimenting
> you and accept their comment by saying
> *thank you.* Now who wants to begin the
> celebrations?"

Hands shoot up.

The MCs use the roster list to check off the audiences'
celebrations, giving gentle reminders to make eye contact, to
say *thank you.* The compliments continue until the bell rings.

> "Let's give a round of applause for our
> MCs!" I say. "Have a great weekend," I say a
> little louder as students round up the
> applause, gather their books, and exit class.

Peer Conferring Protocol (Formal)

Daily, you likely use informal sharing protocols like think-pair-
share. This is great and important for students to share often as
discussed above in the daily protocol.

We do peer conferencing informally quite often (students
trying out drafts or quick-writes with a neighbor), but I've
found that arranging a formal peer feedback day can support
writers who are ready to revise their poems. This is an ideal
time at midterm or end of the semester when you invite
students to create portfolios and do reflections on their writing
development. This formal experience also helps writers by
requiring them to really listen, attend to a fellow writer, and be
the reader. In this stance, they offer a service to their classmates
while also benefiting from their fellow writers' successes and
struggles. Essentially, all writing pieces are Mentor Poems

because every writer is an expert in their topic and voice. The process is simple:

- Arrange the class into groups of 3.
- Hand out a guide like the green one below — a notebook or sticky notes work well, too.
- Ask every writer to reread their piece silently or in a whisper and write one part on which they'd like feedback.
- Then, the first person should tell the writing group his/her needs before reading aloud the piece.
- The writing group can take notes, but the writing group mustn't see the piece –just listen to the flow, and follow the ideas. The feedback is not about grammar or proofreading.
- Finally, the writer asks the group for feedback and takes notes him/herself: 1) What stood out to you as a reader/listener? 2) What feedback do you have based on my initial request? and 3) What are you still wondering about, would like to hear more about, or would you like me to make more clear/or less obvious in my revision?
- Repeat the process for each group member, and then make time for revisions.

All of this presumes the writer is publishing his/her work, sharing it beyond the notebook (virtual or digital). When we write to inform, teach, entertain, and communicate, a reader-audience is implied. We have readers in mind, so it makes sense to try it out on one or two just in case it does not inform, teach, entertain, or communicate as we intended. Of course, writers may not want to hear from said implied reader, may simply want to put that work into the world without interference. I get that.

Essentially, feedback is a reader holding up a mirror for you, the writer. The feedback comes with a reader's prior experiences, familiarity with the topic, and reading stance. It is up to the writer what she does with the reflection, which may be crystal clear and may be distorted.

(Un)Grading

While we are focused on the sort of learning that defies measurement, we understand that you will likely have to do some sort of accounting of the time you and your students are spending on poetry. For sure, you can point to many reading, writing, speaking, and listening standards that you are supporting in this practice, but you must also communicate this evidence in your learning management system (LMS), such as Canvas, Blackboard, Google Classroom (or whatever has become the new system). Parents and students check the grade portal, and you may need to enter something like two grades a week.

We don't want to talk about grades, but it is part of school culture. Sarah has written about what she calls "the ghosts of grading's past" and how so much of our learning mindset is wrapped up in past grading experiences. Our writing identity is also bound to this if we receive messages that we are bad at writing (spelling or grammar) or a great writer (neat handwriting). We think you can ethically evaluate these poetry experiences while following your school grading practices to some degree. At the heart of upgrading is a shift in how you talk about grading and assessment. First, don't grade based on how many poems a student wrote if they followed the prompt, or if their handwriting is legible. Now, we will explore thematic analysis, reflection, and portfolio as healthier, authentic options.

The end of a term or midterm should be, in our view, a time to celebrate learning, reflect on growth, and give thanks. Thus, you must first set aside a couple of days at the end of the quarter for thematic analysis and reflection at which time you will talk to students one-on-one and try to do all of "that" (celebrate, reflect, and give thanks) in under five minutes. It may seem like an inconsequential length of time, but we think it makes all the difference in our learning relationships.

Peer Conferring Protocol for the Writer

Writer's Name:_____

Listeners' Name(s): #1_____ &

#2_____

Instructions: Before you read or ask for feedback let your listener know what you need from them: *One thing I really want your feedback on is (my opening, closing, organization, transition, etc.).*

Now, read your writing to the listener. If you notice anything you'd like to change as you read, feel free to stop and make that revision.

When you are done reading, ask the listen some questions and write notes of their responses to help you with your revisions:

    1. What stood out to you as a reader/listener?

#1

#2

    2. What feedback do you have based on my initial request?

#1

#2

    3. What are you still wondering about, would like to hear more about, or would you like me to make more clear/or less obvious in my revision?

#1

#2

Thank the listeners. Invite them to share their writing with you.

Thematic Analysis and Reflection

For the first time, you, dear teacher, should model the process outlined below. You want to do the sort of writerly reflection you want students to do, and your think-aloud process will be helpful. They will also see the messiness of you doing the work, and this will make you more compassionate as you witness and support your students doing this very high-level thinking.

Here are some steps:
1. Ask students to look at their completed table of contents (or more accurately fill out their table of contents because this falls by the wayside often).
2. Invite students to notice the themes in their poetic choices: what topics did they write about, what forms did they tend to write in, and what sorts of ratings did they give? Can the students find any patterns or themes in their table of contents?
3. Then, have students read through some of their poems and see if they notice patterns in the length, form, revisions, editing, drawings, etc. What do they see in their writing approaches and processes?
4. Finally, invite students to write a reflection using any or all of the following prompts.

Choose one you can thinking deeply about. Write in your journal to prepare for your conference.

1. Of all that you've done, created, discovered this quarter, what are you most proud of (for reading, for writing)?
2. What is something that was a struggle but that you worked through to find success (in reading, in writing)?
3. What are you noticing in yourself as a reader, writer, thinker that is becoming stronger?
4. What are you noticing in books/stories that you read and write that you didn't notice before (that you learned from what we've been reading, writing)?
5. If you could do any assignment or experience over to do and be better, what would you do differently and why?
6. Come up with your own question related to reading/writing and respond.

Conferences

As students work on their reflections, you can call students over for 5 minutes at a time to discuss one or two of their reflections and point to poems that they are especially proud of.

While you are conferring, students should be working on an alternative project, which may be to type in their favorite poems into their own anthology or to look for images to put alongside their poems in a personal book.

We talk about their reflection; we decide on a final grade; and I thank them for their contributions to our learning community. Each student offers something unique to our class, and the conference is an opportunity for me to share my observations and gratitude.

Students tell me that they struggled to find time to read but figured out a routine that worked for them. They tell me they are noticing authorial choices in the books they read. They tell me they are learning how to make their stories come alive. They tell me they are writing because they love it and not because it's an assignment. They tell me that they know they are writers because their classmates laugh at their stories, compliment their word choice, and ask them to write a sequel.

A conference should be a conversation to uncover how students see themselves as readers and writers through and beyond the artifacts or evidence. I want insight into their thinking and self-perception, and I want to share with them what I am learning about who they are and are becoming as readers, writers, and class members so that we can build on those experiences.

Concluding Thoughts

As we wrap up this introductory chapter, you now have the foundational tools to embark on a poetic journey with your students. From setting up your notebooks, whether paper or digital, to guiding your class through a brief yet impactful poetic experience, you're equipped to start the school year or jump in at any point with confidence and enthusiasm. This chapter has also provided you with a sample lesson to spark creativity, strategies for fostering a sense of belonging through open mic sessions, and a structured peer conferring protocol to enhance collaborative learning. By embracing the principles of poetry, you are poised to create a learning environment where students are supported in a way that prioritizes growth and understanding. Remember, this journey is all about the students — enjoy the process and let the poetic moments in the chapters that follow inspire and elevate your teaching.

Chapter 2: Celebrating Self(s)

Dear Teacher,

Well, you're here. You've attended all the beginning-of-the-year required PD, your rosters have been updated, and your desks have been labeled. Bulletin boards are up. The classroom library, if you are allowed to have one, is fairly organized, possibly for the last time this year. Your ice-breaker activities are ready to go. Students are about to arrive. Now what?

Creating a classroom community is of utmost importance, but it sure can't be done in one day. Successful teachers know that building community must be done daily through self-inquiry. What better way than to share experiences through poetry? The poetry prompts we provide for the beginning of the school year encourage our writers to dig deep to explore who they are in a caring and nurturing classroom environment. We have sequenced the topics in a way that encourages the writer to be gentle with themselves and others while the classroom community develops by learning to honor the individual. After all, sharing who they are and what is important to them is what makes students feel as if they belong and are safe.

In this section, students will be given inquiry opportunities to help them write about their identities. Students can consider how they are similar to and different from their classmates. We start the school year with poetic forms that will help students ease into writing poetry. Additionally, our prompts will guide them gently as they learn to trust and be vulnerable with their writings. We encourage you to give students agency when it comes to sharing. Students will quickly recognize that as individuals, they bring their own unique experiences and expertise to the space. The writing they do in this unit will lead nicely into the next topic, which is "Becoming Us."

Peace, *Sarah, Mo, & Maureen*

1. Why Thursday?
Original prompt by Anna J. Small Roseboro

Inspiration

Anna asks us to reflect on the days of the week and consider which day of the week is the best for each of us.

Process

After students choose their favorite day of the week, they will write an **acrostic poem** about their day. Write the letters of the day of the week down the left side of the page, then using words that begin with that letter, write the lines of the poem that show and tell why that day is good for the writer. This format will likely be a familiar one to students. You can challenge students to write their acrostic poems by writing their favorite day down the right margin of the paper so that each letter will become the last letter of the words in that line.

Mentor Poem

"Why Thursday?" by Anna J. Small Roseboro

Thursdays are my best days
How can that be, you ask? It's about finalizing an assigned task.
Under the gun to finish a project, I have one more day.
Rest and relaxation for the weekend are on the way.
Sunday's coming! That's my day to worship and pray.
Doing my work by Thursday to turn it in on Friday
Always seemed to climax on this blest day
Yielding to tasks that must be done, then comes the weekend of
fun!

2. All Things Cheese
Original prompt by Tammi Belko

Inspiration

Tammi notes that many of her reluctant writers can get overwhelmed with too many free-write or choice options in writing workshops, but they are often motivated by writing poetry. Perhaps the rhythmic patterns, structures, or brevity contribute to student success in poetry writing. Tammi found inspiration in poet G. K. Chesterton's comment, "Poets have been mysteriously silent on the subject of cheese." An inspirational poem Tammi suggests is Benjamin Garcia's "Bliss Point or What Can Best Be Achieved by Cheese," which can be found at Poets.org.

Process

Begin by brainstorming:
- List attributes of cheese or any favorite food.
- Consider how this food makes you feel.
- What connections do you have with this food?
- When and with whom do you consume this food?
- What forms does this food take?
- Can it be used to make other foods?
- Is it best paired with another food?

Ideas
- Incorporate some **alliteration** and **personification**
- Try an **extended Haiku**.
- Use Garcia's poem as a template.
- Choose any form you want to experiment with or write in free verse.

Mentor Poem

"All Things Cheese" by Tammi Belko

The thing about cheese
It fulfills every craving
Breakfast, lunch, dinner …
Cheddar on my eggs
The best burrito breakfast
Scrambled perfection!

Provolone cheese, Yum!
Best bubbling in my pizza
Or a string cheese snack

Mozzarella cheese
Layered on my lasagna
Sprinkled on salad

But don't stop just, yet
Grate gruyere, crumble some feta
Top your veggies, too!

3. Genetic Cinquains
Original prompt by Jessica Wiley

Inspiration
Did you know that at least 615 national holidays can be celebrated in the United States in September? These include National No Rhyme or Reason Day, Happy Cat Month, Self-Improvement Month, and even Eat an Extra Dessert Day. Jessica invites us to seize the day and celebrate who we are. Have students choose a holiday to celebrate, or allow them to look at the list of holidays celebrated on their birthdays. The holiday they choose should allow them to celebrate themselves in some way. You can find a list of holidays at the National Today Calendar.

Process
Have students brainstorm a list of their qualities and features, flaws and all! These features are genetically unique, and original to each student, and will help them write today's poem. Today's poetry form is the **cinquain**, a poem or stanza composed of five lines. Two types are highlighted today, the **American Cinquain** and the **Didactic Cinquain**, with two examples provided. The American Cinquain is an unrhymed five-lined poetic form with 22 syllables:
- Line One- two syllables
- Line Two- four syllables
- Line Three-six syllables
- Line Four-eight syllables
- Line Five-two syllables

The Didactic Cinquain is often used in elementary classrooms.
- Line One: One word (a noun, the subject of the poem)
- Line Two: Two words (adjectives that describe the subject)
- Line Three: Three words (-ing action verbs–participles–that relate to the subject)
- Line Four: Four words (a phrase or sentence that relates feelings about the subject)
- Line Five: One word (a synonym or a word that sums it up)

Mentor Poems

"American Cinquain" by Jessica Wiley

Light-Bright
Left-handed child
Full lips, rounded waistline
Sandy hair streaked with gray wisdom
Wide-eyed

"Didactic Cinquain" by Jessica Wiley

Jessica
Trustworthy, Dedicated
Caring, Adapting, Smiling, Encouraging
Loyal and overcommitted spirit
Theia

4. The Skinny

Original prompt by Glenda Funk

Inspiration

Glenda found her inspiration in Ezra Pound's brief poem "In a Station of the Metro." The poem, although only two lines and 14 words long, has striking imagery. A **Skinny poem** uses the less is more approach to writing. A Skinny poem invites us to construct vivid images with few words.

Process

Have students brainstorm a list of issues, current events, or topics important to them. Or they might find inspiration in a moment from their day, a holiday event, a work of art, a pet. Capture the moment in a sentence. Try to avoid using "being" verbs, which create passivity in our writing. Make a list of possible words to add to the poem. Play with the order. Skinnys have eleven lines, but nine of the lines contain only one word each. Only lines one and ten deviate from the one-word line length. Consider numbering the lines as you compose.

- Line 1 begins with a strong image;
- lines 2-10 build on the image in line 1;
- lines 6 and 10 repeat the word used in line 2; and
- line 11 must be comprised of all words in line 1, but the words may be ordered in any way the writer desires.
- Remember lines 2, 6, and 10 repeat.

Notice how the repeated lines (words) reinforce the image.

Mentor Poem

"Vaccinated" by Denise Krebs

I winced but smiled with the second dose.
Wondering
Hoping
Dreaming
Drifting
Wondering
Mutants
Spreading
Wildfire
Wondering
With the second dose, I smiled but winced.

5. Where I'm From
Original prompt by Mo Daley

Inspiration

Childhood can make us think of magical times, poignant memories, or even anxiety-ridden days. Today let's write a poem filled with imagery that shows the reader what our childhood was like. "Where I'm From," by George Ella Lyon has inspired similar poems for years. Imagine the discoveries your students will make about themselves and one another as they write and share their poems. You can also find online templates that support writers in accessing details.

Process

Brainstorm a list of moments, places, sounds, smells, and sights that resonate with you from childhood. Focus on poetic language such as **simile, metaphor, imagery, or onomatopoeia**. Write an "I Am From" poem that shows the reader who you really are.

Mentor Poem

"I am" by Mo Daley

I am from the clamor and clatter of
        doors slamming shut and creeping open.
I am from, "Whose shoes are these?!?" and
        "Hurry up and get to the table!"
I am from suburbia, where everyone knew me
        and I knew everyone.
I am from nightly dinners at the kitchen table
        seated on the bench
        made for three little ones.
I am from Ryan's Trick Shop, where we would
        all buy Swedish Fish for a quarter
        on Fridays
        on the way home from school.
I am from freshly cut grass and
        burning leaves assaulting our nostrils.
I'm from the unrelenting BUZZ BUZZ BUZZ of the
        17-year cicadas
        desperately trying to attract a mate before it's too
late.
I am from a house with one bathtub,
        two toilets, and 22 hands
        pounding on the bathroom doors
        each fighting for a few moments of privacy.
I am sympathy and trust and care and love
        And, "I got you, no matter where you are or what
you need."
I am from
DonLorettaSteveBrianChrisTommyTimmyBillyBobbyArM
o.

6. Lists
Original prompt by Linda Mitchell

Inspiration

Linda suggests we peek into our writer's notebooks or any other place we write and peruse our lists. What jumps out at us?

Process

Today let's look for one word to "write along" with. Let's use the Lift-a-Word strategy and either randomly or intentionally choose a word to write about. Today's poem can be in any format. Just write and see where our chosen word takes us.

Mentor Poem

"Wishing Well Price List" by Linda Mitchell

Daisy petals	..............love and love-not
Maple seedling	............for a sweet winter
Penny	...........one hello from heaven
Two chestnuts	...........one measure of honesty & strength
Spiderweb	............mysterious adventure
Handful of acorns	..........good health
Four leaf clover	............good luck
Horseshoe	............double clover luck
Five smooth stones	.........weapons to fight giants
One full dream-catcher	.........room size mural with portal to the future
Wren feathers	..........safe hearth
Eyelash and one long-held breath	.............patience on the wait for wishes to come true and come home

7. Apology Poem
Original prompt by Allison Berryhill

Inspiration

Allison suggests we use William Carlos Williams's short poem "This Is Just to Say" for our inspiration. Allison notes that Williams's poem is only 12 lines long and consists of three four-line stanzas. No line has more than five syllables. Yet the visual, tactile, and gustatory imagery of those cold plumbs serves as one of the most recognized **allusions** in poetry!

Process

Here are two ways to use this poem as a springboard:

1) What do you need to SAY? Here is your chance to say it. Begin your poem/note with "This is just to say," and get it said, loud and proud, or simply and softly. It's your note.

2) The last lines of Williams's poem ask for forgiveness, then settle back on the delicious pleasure of eating the plums that were not his. How sincere is this apology? Write a 12-line non-apology to someone or something. Offer the apology, but then settle back on the pleasure derived from your offending action, as Williams seems to do.

Mentor Poem

"This is just to say" by Allison Berryhill

I have forgotten
your name
that was on
my roster in 2006

and which
you were probably
expecting
me to remember

Forgive me
you were once my student
my focus

Next, please?

8. What I Want Is
Original prompt by Allison Berryhill

Inspiration

Allison cites C. G. Hanzlicek's poem "What I Want Is," as inspiration for today's prompt. The poem is a series of two-lined stanzas that uses line breaks and **enjambment**, or the continuation of a sentence or clause across a line break, effectively.

Process

Begin with a declaration of a want, and allow your mind to explore the imagery related to your "want" with prepositional phrases as Hanzlicek does: beneath that hill, in the pond, on the mud. Consider matching Hanzlicek's number of stanzas, eleven, –or go rogue. You might conclude your poem by counting, as Hanzlicek does: Coyote 1, Coyote 2. I have used this poem as a model many times, and it never fails to elicit successful poems. In this version, I went with my fashion envy!

Mentor Poem

"What I Want Is" by Allison Berryhill

What I want is
That mouse-soft sweater

Kristina is wearing.
"You can feel it"

She offers when I
Say I like it.

What I want is
Brynna's leafy lacy shirt

The color of ferns
Resting against mossy stones

And hair like hers
Over there

And those leggings
those boots

The cat-eye glasses
Resting on the bridge of that nose

Because English
Teachers know how

To rock Educator style
On the NCTE
Runway

Work it Work it.

9. My Best Parts
Original prompt by Sarah Donovan

Inspiration

Something Sarah has noticed about teaching is that her identity tends to get wrapped up, even defined by her role in the lives of students. She sometimes forgets who she, Sarah, is — the quirks and gifts that she has carried with her heart, mind, and body. Is this true for you? Today, we invite you to think about yourself and tell us about your best part, the best part of you — the you who you've always been.

Process

Choose one of these to get you started or try a stanza for each – 3 or 4 lines that rhyme or just have a similar meter (syllables per line):
- describe what your best part looks like — size, color, shape, texture
- tell what your best part allows you to do that you enjoy
- tell who gave you this part, was it inherited, developed/earned through experience or necessity
- state the words, the best part of me, somewhere in your poem

Mentor Poem

"The Best Part" by Sarah Donovan

The best part of me
no one can see.
It is not my nose, my nails, or my knees.
It is not my face, my forearms, or my feet.

The best part of me comes alive when I day dream.
Ideas for world peace.
Imaginings for stories.
Words to assuage pain.
Lessons to connect us.

The best part of me that stirs in a day dream
might just mean
that I am not listening
to you
And for that
I am sorry.

When you catch me staring off into space,
ask me what I am thinking.
I will gladly bring you into my dream
and the best part
of me.

10. I Love Me!
Original prompt by Jessica Wiley

Inspiration

Jessica remembers being a teen and falling in love with poetry to try and impress boys. She was pleasantly surprised at a recent student-led parent-teacher conference when her 10-year-old daughter, Katalyn, shared a poem she wrote that showed her vulnerability, flaws, and self-love. Katalyn's class used Eloise Greenfield's poem, "By Myself," as a Mentor Poem. You can read Katalyn's poem below.

Process

Before writing, brainstorm a list of things that come to your mind. Who are you? What are you made of? Who or what do you most resemble or relate to? Think of emotions, colors, sounds of nature, or inanimate objects that define you. Make a list and play on these words. Using the template below and possibly a mirror, reflect deeply, speaking on behalf of your inner self. Make yourself come alive! Follow this 15 line template:

- The first two lines are:
    "When I'm by myself
    And I close my eyes"
- The next eight lines:
    - Rhyme
    - Begin with" I'm".
- The last five lines are:
    "I'm whatever I want to be
    An anything I care to be
    And when I open my eyes
    What I care to be
    Is me"

Mentor Poem

"When I'm By Myself" by Katalyn Wiley

When I'm by myself
And I close my eyes
I'm a flame
I'm rain
I'm ice
I'm nice
I'm an explosion
I'm a motion
I'm trouble
I'm a bubble
I'm a whatever I want to be
An anything I care to be
And when I open my eyes
What I care to be
Is me.

11. Memories
Original by Andy Schoenborn

Inspiration

Life comes at us fast. Without a doubt there are hills, valleys, and plateaus. On occasion these moments make for a memorable (if not defining) experience – one that is remembered throughout a person's life. For many, the senior year of high school is ripe for remembering and celebrating. Let's choose a moment or series of moments from your senior year of high school that captures your fondest memories.

Process

Take a few minutes and write down a series of memories from your last year in elementary school, middle school, or high school -- or even think back to kindergarten graduation.

Start with the year you "graduated" to give the poem context.

Don't worry about rhyme or chronological order, just weave in the highlights of the memories you will always carry with you.

End the poem by sharing what you thought your future would hold during that time.

Mentor Poem

"1978" by Allison Berryhill

1978 smelled like Marlboro Lights
Diana's Monte Carlo
warm Budweiser
musk perfume.

1978 tasted like two all-beef patties
special sauce lettuce cheese pickles onions
on a sesame seed bun
and syrupy sloe gin fizz.

1978 felt like that soft blue sweater
from Mitch.
My mother said I couldn't keep it;
no boy should give a girl a sweater.

1978 sounded like slamming doors
and cussing and
Bob Seger pounding on the 8-track
drowning the last of
my childhood.

12. Ego and Homage
Original post by Barb Edler

Inspiration

Barb cites Nikki GIovanni's "Ego Tripping" and Lucille Clifton's "Homage to My Hips" as inspiration for today's prompt. Barb asks us to look at Giovanni's rich, honest language that creates strong images and impressions. Giovanni also makes wonderful use of **hyperbole** in the poem. Alternatively, we can ask students to consider paying homage to a particular trait they possess as Lucille Clifton does in her poem.

Process

This type of writing activity might be meaningful for students to reflect on their own identities, but as an alternative, it can be a useful character exploration activity if students write an "ego" or "homage" poem based on literary figures. Consider exploring your own uniqueness and use hyperbole to share your strength, wisdom, beauty, talent, etc. For Barb's poem, she celebrated the color of her eyes while incorporating some allusion.

Mentor Poem

"My Green Eyes" by Barb Elder

My green eyes
Are darker than
The emerald sea
As piercing as
The summer's sun
Stronger than Odysseus;
Patient as his
Poor wife Penelope;
Sexy as the
Sirens' hypnotic songs
Divining the truth
Of ancient mysteries
And tantalizing as
A jazzy tune

13. Memory Snapshot
Original post by Kim Johnson

Inspiration

Sharing memories, moments, messages…taking the hand of the reader and saying, "Come with me. Have you ever….?" As writers, we are diviners of stories that need to be told. Stories validate, motivate, educate. They have the power to change, tell the truth, call out injustice, conjure the past and take us back there, bring back lost loved ones, and sing the unsung heroes in ways that regular prose cannot – yet the prose poems and flash essays in *You are No Longer in Trouble* by Nicole Stellon O'Donnell burst wide open, exploding with vivid memories.

Process

Choose any form of verse today that shares a vivid memory story – perhaps one that evokes pain, humor, fear, love, or any other strong emotion that still lives on…. dive into the pool of memories that need to be told – – and bring it to the surface with words and images!

Mentor Poem

"Spring Sleepover" by Betsy Jones

tucked under
a cotton blanket
we swing
on my front porch
we whisper
best friend secrets
between bites
of chocolate graham crackers
we wish
on the stars
one for each jewel
in Orion's Belt

14. The Way I Felt
Original post by Kim Johnson

Inspiration

Kim was inspired by the poem "The Way I Felt" in Jason Reynolds' multi-award-winning novel *Long Way Down*. Reynolds is the National Ambassador of Young People's Literature.

Process

If you are feeling nostalgic, keep the past tense and direct address. If you are feeling connected to the present, move to the present tense. The "I" need not be you, but could invite another perspective in human form or an abstract concept like Love, Joy, Grief, or Regret.

Mentor Poem

"The Way I" by Kim Johnson

The Way I
felt when your
tail thumped three
times was heartbroken.

I never had
a dog as
loyal as you.

I stood on
the front porch
waiting for you
to look up
but you were
too weak to
lift your head.

Three tail thumps.
And I understood.

It was time.

"Just this side
of Heaven is
a place called…

Rain…bow…bridge"

*Quoted lines are attributed to Paul C. Dahm from the
original "Rainbow Bridge Poem."

15. Something You Should Know
Original prompt by Emily Yamasaki

Inspiration

There are many mundane moments and daily actions in our lives. These may seem less noteworthy, but upon closer inspection, you may find that they shed some light as to who we are as individuals. Clint Smith's poem below sheds light on a being in a way that is subtle and powerful : "Something You Should Know/is that as a kid, I once worked at a pet store./I cleaned the cages/of small animals like turtles, hamsters, /rabbits, and hermit crabs./I watched the hermit crab..." Notice the pattern of "I" and action words (worked, cleaned, watched) with very specific details.

Process

Make a list of places you have worked or lived. Or make a list of the chores you have in your home or neighborhood. Choose one that stands out to you that you'd like to explore today. Try Clint Smith's repetition and vivid verbs.

Mentor Poem

"Something You Should Know" by Emily Yamasaki

is that when I was young, I once worked as a Kelly's
Coffee barista.
I greeted patrons
of all ages, baked blueberry scones, and
of course, made caffeinated beverages.
I tamped the espresso neat
and tidy, like a hockey puck, into the wand
leaving zero trace of crumb on the edges.
Espresso grind is notoriously messy,
Which only gave me more resolve to
meticulously pack it, manage it, control it.
Perhaps that i when I became
obsessed with having a spot for everything.
Perhaps that is why, even now,
when I get the desperate urge to
leave a crumb,
I'm afraid so
I sweep them all neatly away.

References

Belko, T. (2022, April 22). All things cheese. Ethical ELA. https://www.ethicalela.com/all-things-cheese/

Berryhill, A. (2020, Feb. 12). Apology poem. Ethical ELA. https://www.ethicalela.com/february-day-3-5-apology-poem/

Berryhill, A. (2020, Feb. 16. What I want is... Ethical ELA. https://www.ethicalela.com/february-day-2-5-what-i-want-is/

Daley, M. (2019, August 21). Where I'm from. Ethical ELA. https://www.ethicalela.com/august-3-5-day-writing-challenge/

Edler, B. (2020, Sept. 20). Ego and homage. Ethical ELA. https://www.ethicalela.com/septembers-openwrite-ego-and-homage/

Funk, G. (2021, April 10). The skinny poem. Ethical ELA. https://www.ethicalela.com/10-30-the-skinny/

Johnson, K. (2020, May 18). The way I felt. Ethical ELA. https://www.ethicalela.com/may-openwrite-the-way-i-felt/

Johnson, K. (2021, March 13). Weddings at recess. Ethical ELA. https://www.ethicalela.com/weddings-at-recess/

Krebs, D. (2021, April 10). The skinny poem. Ethical ELA. https://www.ethicalela.com/10-30-the-skinny/

Mitchell, L. (2020, June 20). Lists. Ethical ELA. https://www.ethicalela.com/june-openwrite-lists/

Morice, S. (2019, Nov. 10). Rituals/Traditional moments. Ethical ELA. https://www.ethicalela.com/november-1-5-day-writing-challenge/

Roseboro, A. (2022, April 15). Why Thursday. Ethical ELA. https://www.ethicalela.com/why-thursday/

Schoenborn, A. (2019, Oct. 14). Senior year. Ethical ELA. https://www.ethicalela.com/october-2-5-day-writing-challenge/

Wiley, J. (2022, April 28). By my self-love. Ethical ELA. https://www.ethicalela.com/by-my-self-love/

Wiley, J. (2023, April 25). Genetic cinquain. Ethical ELA. https://www.ethicalela.com/genetic-cinquains/

Yamasaki, E. (2023, April 8). Something you should know. Ethical ELA. https://www.ethicalela.com/something-you-should-know/

Resources

Reynolds, J. (2017). *Long way down*. Simon and Schuster.

Chapter 3: Becoming Us

Dear Teacher,

You are well on your way now with poetry. Your notebook and your students' notebooks have quite a few poems, which may be 15 times as many poems as you have written in your life. Let's take a moment to celebrate that.

And you have likely figured out that the paper notebooks are becoming an important object and space of belonging for you and your students. However, you may have allowed students to take their notebooks with them and realized this has caused a problem because they "left it at home" or 'lost it." We hope you will consider keeping the notebooks in the classroom and offer those students an extra notebook to keep at home if possible. On the other hand, the digital notebooks may be working out well, if you went that way. They are likely not lost, but you may find that students are not making progress as you liked or getting lost searching for poems or maybe even using ChatGPT instead of writing their own poems. So this is a good time to adjust your routines or have a meeting with your students to get their feedback on how to adapt the practice in ways that serve your community of learners.

This section is all about community. If the time of year is September and October maybe leaning into November, you are likely to see Halloween themes popping up at your school or in your community. This is a good time to consider variances in your classroom and welcome students to write about their different autumn memories and traditions. Maybe students celebrate or will want to celebrate Dia de Los Muertos and write poems for a class ofrenda. Maybe students will want to poem into arguments around Columbus Day and Indigenous People's Day. Ramadan practices shift, so fasting may be something your students are practicing and will want to write about or share with peers. The traditions of the fall season may welcome distractions or complicate school and/or students' lives, so the poetry in this section can surface commonalities and variances of this time of year, which can go a long way in nurturing a sense of trust and belonging in your classroom.

In essence, this is a time for students to get to know one another and do a little practice with perspective taking to nurture compassion and empathy.

In Matthew Kay's book *Not Light But Fire*, he writes about, among other things, safe spaces. He says that teachers cannot declare a space is safe. It takes everyone in the class to nurture a place of safety for critical conversations and sharing of our lives in ways that cultivate safety and an inclusive, affirming learning environment. We hope you find these prompts to support such an endeavor of belonging.

One more reminder: be gentle with yourself. October, in particular, is a difficult month for teachers, so we hope poetic thinking will serve your heart and mind in gentle ways.

Peace,
Sarah, Maureen, & Mo

1. Poetic Drive-Bys
Original prompt by Bryan Ripley Crandall

Inspiration

National Book Award Winner Ruth Stone was known, in her poetry workshops, to stop a student after a reading to say, "Oh, you've written a poem-poem," which she explained as, "a gift to the universe."

Our teacher-poet-friend Bryan Ripley Crandall likes to assign students to think of a person, place, or thing worthy of a poem, and to write as if making an offering. The poem becomes a gift.. At his Kentucky high school, students used to call these "poetic drive-bys" and would chalk their poems on sidewalks or write them for strangers to find in the mall. Community gifts (not GIFs). One young man delivered his poetry to fast food employees around town.

You can see where we are going with this, right? Your students will write a poem in their paper or digital notebook, but you could also take students outside with some chalk today or set them on a mission to deliver their poems to friends, teachers, school staff, family and neighbors more broadly.

Process

Write today's poem for someone else: the boy who bags your groceries, the neighbor who walks by your front window every day, that friend who has been on your mind. Craft the poem to be left for another to unwrap (a gift that we all need).

Mentor Poem

"Deliveries" by b.r.crandall

You don't belong to us,
these porches of boxes,
driveways, & sidewalks –
yet, you bring stamped smiles
to our criss-crossing streets,
always carrying that satchel of language
over your shoulder:
sales, news, bills, birthday cards –
a correspondence of snails
assigned to chase Paul Revere.

We see you in the morning
working with packaged purpose,
eyes on lookout
for fuzz-nuggets
yanking idiots like me
at the end
of their ropes.

You might as well be my mom,
aunt, therapist,
reader of Tarot cards
who explained to me that death
is just like Publisher's Clearing House.

Karal asked me to write you this poem
in exchange for the milkbones –

Joy, she says, comes from a delivered gesture.
Yours, hers, mine.

That's why I let her lick
the envelope.

2. When You Need a Break
Original prompt by Leilya Pitre

Inspiration
It is early October, and fall is upon us in some form or another. Maybe there are leaves on the ground. Maybe there are Halloween decorations in the stores. But school has been in session for over a month, and you are likely feeling the shift from the honeymoon stage of a new school year into the infamous teacher slump of October. Today, we ask you to name it with your students and invite them to go for a walk, a figurative walk to your/their place of comfort. A walk is time for reflection and relaxation. It is time to accept, forget, and forgive. It is time to recharge and restore your balance. An inspiration for today's poetry writing comes from many poets, among those are a few favorites that you can pull from the web and tape on the walls of your room or invite students to tape into their notebooks: Elizabeth Bishop's "The End of March," Robert Frost's "A Late Walk," Gary Snyder's "A Walk," and Theodore Roethke's "A Field of Light."

Process
There are different ways to write a walk poem:

- You may write about different things that attract your attention during the walk;
- You may write about the walk that resulted in some important personal revelation;
- You may write about the walk into the past—a place or time—that brings you comfort, delight, or help face struggles;
- You may write a poem that mirrors the length, style, and shape of the actual walk.
- Teacher, you may invite your students to go for a walk outside around the school. Let your office staff know that you are taking your crew for a walk around the parking lot. Ask students to talk about a place that brings them comfort and how to get there.

There is no specific pattern, count of syllables, or rhyme requirements. Freestyle! Today's writing aims to clear your mind of frustrations, annoyances, and anxiety. Let go of your stress by walking (literally or figuratively), visiting your place of comfort. For our teacher-poet-friend, this place is her childhood home in Crimea, Ukraine. We share this poem in its entirety in memory of Leilya's friends and family impacted by the war in Ukraine.

Mentor Poem

"Finding Peace" by Leilya Pitre

When I need a break,
    I walk home — to my haven,
a place where my soul finds peace —
 Mom's soothing voice shields me
from all the pain in the world.
I close my eyes and see
    an old Post Office building —
newspapers, greeting cards,
    envelopes, stamps, and
faint scent of sealing wax.
An acacia tree alley outside with
    delicate fragrance of white blossoms
trails up to the central square
    opening to the movie theater on the right,
Court House and the department store on the left.
Seven minutes along Matrosova Street —
 Daisies, roses, lilies, and zinnias in front yards —
quilted blankets of red, yellow, orange, blue,
    and every color in between followed
by vibrant greenery of apricot, peach, and cherry trees.
Here is a special corner whirling
    toward my favorite place —
a bench under the patulous mulberry tree,
    where neighborhood kids gathered
to share stories, jokes, and songs.
A few more steps, and I breathe in home,
    lavish grape vines over the tall iron-wrought arch
meet me with clusters of purple cabernet.
    Mom turns her head, eyes wide, smiling: "Daddy, look who
is here!"

3. Perspective Poem
Original prompt by Judi Opager

Inspiration
Our inspiration today is perspective-taking. It's not always easy to consider the perspective of another person because we have to do a lot of inferring and that may also promote stereotyping or assumptions. Perspective-taking can be a start at understanding others.

Our teacher-friend, Judi, wanted to understand what was going through her mother's eyes when she left the family. From many years of teaching, we all know that our students come from diverse family structures: single-parent (divorced, never married), foster parent(s), adoptive parent(s), blended, LGBTQ+, and non-parent-relative(s) as guardians (e.g., grandparents, aunt). Taking on the perspective of family members can be therapeutic; still, we know many of our students have found families—friends, community members, pets—who feel like home, so some perspective-taking can nurture those relationships, too.

Process
Today, we are writing a poem from the perspective of a family member, however we define family -- and from the first person point of view. Step into their shoes. What do you see? What do you learn? Walk through a scene from their memory with you, but from their view. Be tender with your language so as not to cause harm in your representation of them.

Craft tip: Try to use the phrase "I remember." If you repeat this, it is called repetition or anaphora if it repeats at the beginning of a line.

Note: If writing about family feels too hard or you are not ready for that, write from the perspective of an object.

Mentor Poem

"Through the Eyes of Her Mother" by Judi Opager

I remember
laying on the olive green carpet, feeling the pattern beneath my
cheek
Listening to The Beatles on the phonograph.

I remember
"Hey Jude," and how the words washed over me like a scalding
hot shower,
"Take a sad song and make it better."...

I remember
that I had already made my decision to leave
and was mourning the loss…

I remember
moving into the new future
with my old blue suitcase.

I remember
the confusion on my children's faces
as I quietly shut the door after myself.

Mentor Poem

"App" by DeAnna

She presses my face
Waking me yet again
What can she be looking for
Will she find it
Two quick clicks to where it can be found
She logs out and shuts me down

How long until she wakes me again?

4. What About Your Friends
Original prompt by Jessica Wiley

Inspiration

Friends. What about them, right? Well, Bill Withers, Andrew Gold, Marvin Gaye and Tammi Terrell, Randy Newman, The Rembrandts, Dionne Warwick, TLC, The Jackson 5, Whodini, and Zack Attack are just a few artists who have penned friendship songs. These are some of our favorites, but we are sure your students have their own – maybe by Taylor Swift. Today we are inspired by the question of what makes a "good" friend. Our teacher-poet Jessica told us that she grew up having a difficult time making friends because she was quiet and shy. We know that our students' friendships can be strong and fragile.

Process

How do you define friendship? What would an ideal friendship be like for you? What do your friendships currently look like? Do you need to reconcile a friendship? What about making new ones? These are some questions that may open up old wounds and/or heal new ones. To get started, brainstorm a list of songs about friendship and pick one that speaks to you. Borrow a line, chorus, or hook that resonates with you and take off with it. Consider the thoughts and feelings you have when you pick the lines. There's no particular poetic form, just go with the flow. Use the line or lines anywhere in your poem.

Mentor Poem

"Friends Forever" by Jessica Wiley

Elementary school daze
will leave you in a haze.
Coming of age,
too afraid to take the stage.
But then I turn around and there you are,
Rooting me on when the world sees bizarre.
Our past is history, but our story is preserved in amber,
Navigating life with no shoes, maneuvering over the rocks
we clamber.
From meeting interesting strangers to awkward friend
boyfriends,
To years later weddings, graduations, and limited
weekends.
Busyness was the third wheel but no matter how much
time passed,
We picked back up where we left off; roles were never
recast.
TLC sings "Sometimes you have to choose and then you'll
see" (line 38)
It's never a dull moment, forever with the Bestie.

TLC. "What About Your Friends." TLC, 1992,
https://genius.com/Tlc-what-about-your-friends-lyrics

5. What You Missed
Original prompt by Allison Berryhill

Inspiration

If you've accessed Poetry180 (and I suggest you do!), you may be familiar with Tom Wayman's sharp poem "Did I Miss Anything?" Teacher-poet Allison shared another poem with a similar title: "What You Missed That Day You Were Absent from Fourth Grade" by Brad Aaron Modlin. Modlin has a humorous response to students who ask what they missed, starting with "Nothing. When we realized you weren't here/we sat with our hands folded on our desks/in silence." Students love this poem, so we recommend sharing it with them.

Process

Today, write about what you have missed. What might you have missed by skipping/avoiding an activity or situation? What have others missed that you wish they'd experienced? Maybe you have friends or family who refuse to join you in your favorite game or activity. Maybe you never tried something out of fear of failure; what might you have missed? We invite you to explore "something missed" in a literal or imaginary sense. For example, one student wrote to her grandfather on the day after his funeral. Shared with permission.

Mentor Poem

"what you missed the day after" by Genevieve McCalla

you ate the cheesy potatoes at the reception
because they were your favorite

you comforted mom when she cried
because dad had a bottle in his hand

you played checkers with Knox
because he didn't know what was really happening

you straightened up the flag on the coffin
because our eyes were too blurry to notice

you bathed in the cemetery's sunshine
because we had our heads bowed

you sang the hymns in happy tones
because our notes were sad

you smiled down on us always
because you loved us so.

6. I Sing: Writer
Original prompt by Sarah J. Donovan

Inspiration

I Sing: The Body is an anthology of poetry edited by René Saldaña, Jr. The collection of poems thread struggle and celebration within what we are told and what we believe about ourselves. The poems uncover memory and anger and hope. As Sarah read the poetry in this collection, she thought a lot about how our bodies hold and shape so much of who we are.

Our students' (and our own) bodies are changing all the time, and they/we need space to reflect on these changes, appreciating our bodies of yesterday and embracing what our bodies can do today.

Process

Today, we invite you to write about a part of your body (maybe something you inherited) that affords you the strength, agility, flexibility, perspective that makes the world around you a little better. Or consider this part of you in a celebratory way.

What beautiful things do your eyes see? What can you make with your hands? What does your stature allow you to do and see? What can you do for others with your heart?

Take us into a scene when you are using this gift to help another.

Mentor Poem

"Cheek Bones" by Laura Langley

A punctuation mark—
inherited and grown into

like a slash
from temple to mandible

cutting, carving, cleaving
space between equals/
space between lines.

A smile for you.

"hip" by Sarah J. Donovan

hip

a truth—
the shape is inherited.

like a green Katsura leaf
to an apricot heart in autumn,

sway across space
to welcome you.

7. Two-Voice Pop Culture
Original prompt from Sarah J. Donovan

Today is a day for students to work with a partner --
someone perhaps they haven't yet spoken to this school
year (and may not know their name). Paste this chart in
their notebooks and have them talk through each line. Feel
free to skip lines or revise them. Choose categories for the
poem from this (add others as you wish): Books, Artists,
Musicians, Social media, Plays, Genres, Movies, Writing,
Poetry, Activities, Costumes, Clothes, Technology, Games.
(See Appendix for a blank template.)

Mentor Poem

Topic	Jalyn	Suri
I am from (choose category and list a few), (further description)	*I am from Taylor and Billie whose lyrics speak my life.*	*I am from 80s pop, my mom loved Duran, Duran.*
From (choose another category and list two of a category)	*I am from Snapchat, which carries Covid memories.*	*I am from hours of YouTube lash tutorials.*
I am from (describe how you do/consume one of the categories)	*I am from scrolling to avoid eye contact on the bus.*	*I am from Wordle with my sister during Math; she's at college now.*
From (something you learned about life from one of the categories)	*From trips to lakes and caves where we got lost and found our way again.*	*From watching romance movies and hoping for a similar love life.*
I am from (a category that may work as a metaphor for who you are or that has shaped who you are)	*I am from the summer breeze, the exhilaration of discovering something new.*	*I am from change and adaptation, moving from home to home.*
From (a category that you used to escape/feel seen/another verb and how)	*From car rides listening to Imagine Dragons, Adele, and Ariana Grande.*	*From playing with my dog outside until we tired out.*
The (another detail of a category), (its impact on you, why it mattered)	*The taste of lemonade under the summer sun that seemed to last forever.*	*The gloomy sky as we buried him and said our goodbyes.*
From (a specific event, story, time that you engaged in that category)	*From laughter with my best friends at the Greek festival.*	*From helping my mom prepare dinner for my family.*
I'm from (another detail of a category that is important to you that may sum it all up)	*I'm from the blurred photos on my phone – memories of the people I love.*	*I'm from all those moments that make me who I am today.*

8. Scientific Method
Original prompt by Linda Mitchell

Inspiration

The scientific method has five basic steps, plus one feedback step:
1. Make an observation
2. Ask a question
3. Form a hypothesis or testable explanation
4. Make a prediction based on the hypothesis
5. Test the prediction
6. Iterate: use the results to make new hypotheses or predictions.

The scientific process reminds us of poetry. Poets do the work of great scientists: observing, questioning, and predicting–which are vital, although not the total, of the scientific process and poetry.

Process

Re-read the Scientific Process above. Choose one, several, or all the parts to play and poem with. Don't worry about following a specific form because this isn't a specific form. It's a stepping-off place for connecting. Most of all, have fun with words!

Mentor Poem

"After Third Period Chemistry" by Linda Mitchell

Maybe they like me
Do they like me?
If they like me, they will sit with me at lunch
If they sit at my lunch table now, they like me
for sure

You can sit there — if you want
If they like me–like me,
they will sit in the same seat tomorrow.

"Learn How to Fly Drones" by Denise Hill

What happens as more and more
people fly drones?

Amateur drone captains
crowd the sky.

Humbuzz flashes of zip-flying
drones infiltrate our daily lives
like swarming cicadas
whirring overhead.

Step out into the now open air and look up
seize into memory the clear unadulterated expanse
before it becomes obliterated with robotic life.

9. How to Be
Original prompt by Sheri Vasinda

Inspiration

One year Sheri's teaching assignment was changed from self-contained third and fourth grade to fourth grade math and science. She looked for ways to include poetry in both. One of these was through Barry Lane's "How to be…" poems from his book *Reviser's Toolbox*. Her fourth graders loved them, and we found our secondary students did, too. (So do we.)

Process

Look at your heart map from earlier in the school year or think about your favorite topics to talk about or think about. Gather facts on your topic. This is easy after engaging in information writing. The facts are there and writing poetry on the topic of inquiry is a form of text transformation.

- Make a list of 6-10 "good" facts.
- Writing the poem using VERBS: Do this…. Don't…
- Read poems aloud to listen for differences in style and perspective.

Mentor Poem

"How to Be a Breeze" by Sheri Vasinda

Flutter gently, just enough to be a puff or stream of air
Don't blast or whirl.
Rustle the leaves on trees.
Don't bend or break limbs.
Whisper and hum.
Don't shriek or howl.
Waft scents of gardenias and honeysuckle.
Don't blast with stinging sand and debris.
Kiss our faces on warm days.

"How to be a Crazy Cockatiel" by Emma

Pace your cage back and forth
Fly into all the walls
Even though you're very small
Squawk towards the north
And get ready to brawl.

When human comes home
And tries to play ball
Get ready to roam
And make a bird call.

10. Tumble Down Poetry
Original prompt by Andy Schoenborn

Inspiration
We believe a poem rests in wait within each of us. And, yet, for many words are elusive and poems seem out of reach. Oftentimes writers put too much pressure on themselves to find the perfect words or capture the perfect mood. For the small spaces they occupy, poems can cause writers to freeze. To break a poem free try writing a paragraph or two of prose and, then, watch a poem tumble down with this process. You may just find a poem you didn't expect to write!

Process
First, begin with a prompt. Anything will work, but for today let's write about shoes. Please take three minutes and write in prose about a pair of shoes that you'll never forget.

Like this: I bought my first pair of Vans when I was seventeen. They were white-toed and gray with a fresh white wave of leather accenting the sides. Though I was no skater, I had hair long enough for girls to run their fingers through and shoes that were a ready-made canvas for expression. In my room, at friends' homes, on the street, in the park and, even, during school assemblies I would draw, write, and create designs to make these Vans uniquely mine. Checkering the toe like a chess board helped to pass the time. Writing "RESIST" next to a clenched fist on the heel created conversation – so did the heart-shape I colored red.

Then play with the structure and form as a poem tumbles down the page. Look for naturally occurring repetition, alliteration, striking images, and moments of emphasis fit for enjambments.

Mentor Poem

"My First Pair of Vans" by Andy Schoenborn

I bought my first pair of Vans
when I was seventeen.

They were white-toed and gray
with a fresh white wave
of leather accenting the sides.

Though I was no skater,

I had hair long enough
for girls to run their fingers through
and shoes that were a ready-made
canvas for expression.

In my room,
at friends' homes,
on the street,
in the park and, even,
during school assemblies
I would draw,
      write, and
             create designs
to make these Vans
uniquely mine....

11. Quirky Poems
Original poem from Kim Johnson

Inspiration

In the book *Poemcrazy: Freeing Your Life with Words* by Susan Goldsmith Woodridge, Kim felt a deep sense of connection when she read about how Wooldridge's younger brother had made fun of their dad's tacky blue socks. These were nylon, with two black stripes around the top and, upon his return to college, her brother found his dad's ugly socks hiding in his suitcase. The next time he returned home, his brother hid them in the house until they were found by his parents, and returned his way during the next family gathering. The socks once made an appearance next to a rubber chicken in his honeymoon getaway car. Twenty-five years later, they are still exchanging these socks. It brought back memories of Kim's parents, who, up until her mother's death, took turns hiding a Where's Waldo figurine around the house for the other to find.

Process

We all do quirky, bold things that break the ice and bring us closer together. Think of a time that you've done something quirky – – with friends, with family, with students, or even complete strangers. Let's share our quirky exchanges today and whatever emotions they bring – in whatever form of poetry we choose.

Mentor Poem

"Crowns" by Emily Yamasaki

its
just
a mechanical pencil

but

that clear, sleek
stark, white cylindrical
eraser sits on his head like a crown

each of the triplet
pencil princes
take their place on the
thrones inside my bag

never use the eraser
you wouldn't tarnish a crown, would you?

12. Play
Original prompt by Andy Schoenborn

Inspiration

For children play and imagination transform the world into a place they long to be. It seems that, as adults, we can lose sight of the importance of play. The month of October, however, invites students and teachers to reconnect with imaginative play, especially during Halloween and the costumes we wear. It is during this time that many students allow themselves to adopt a new role or identity for a few hours. For this poem, let your imagination soar and try on some new voices or step into a new world.

Process

- As you write, play with visual and auditory imagery to transport your readers into your world.
- For some, it helps to start from the perspective of a child where imagination can flow freely.
- Consider playing with dialogue, onomatopoeia, and capitalization for effect.
- End the poem with gratitude for the gift of imaginative play.

Mentor Poem

"Delayed Coronation" by Glenda Funk

Once upon a time in a land of her mind

Every little girl lived like a Disney
Princess in her imagination.

Courtiers curtsied and consumed crumpets as
They sipped tea from imaginary cups,

Pinky fingers posed in mock monarchy, these
Worlds of Make believe. Father pretended, too,

Until his little princess discovered
Cinderella never lived in Neuschwanstein Castle.

King Ludwig II never finished his home in the
Bavarian Alps. Wars marched on without end.

Only the glass slipper cracked and crumbled. Still,
we gaze through glass ceilings, dreaming.

13. Zip Ode Poem
Original prompt by Mo Daley

The Inspiration

In the summer of 2023, Mo participated in The Poetry Foundation's Summer Poetry Teachers Institute in Miami. It was a wonderfully collaborative experience. One amazing benefit was learning about O, Miami, and their efforts to get poetry into the community. They have done an incredible amount of small and large-scale projects throughout Miami. One that Mo adored was the Zip Ode.

The Process

Think of this poem as an ode to your zip code. All you have to do is write the numbers of your zip code down the left side of your page. That's how many words will be in each line. If you have a 0 in your zip code, think of it as a wild card. You can leave it blank, insert a punctuation mark, add an emoji or a symbol, use any number of words (1-9), or surprise the reader in some way. To insert an emoji in Word, press the Windows logo and the colon. This will bring up the emoji menu.

In the classroom, you may want to offer options, such as using a previous zip code, a grandmother's zip code, or even the zip code of a place students might wish to visit.

Mentor Poem

"Zip Ode" by Mo Daley

6 A sleepy bedroom community just a
0 ☐
4 ride away from Chicago,
5 real star of the show,
2 so close!

14. Masks We Wear
Original prompt from Mo Daley

Inspiration

Mo finds Paul Laurence Dunbar's poem "We Wear the Mask" incredibly moving. It got her thinking about how many of us move through life wearing masks. How well do we know someone? How much of ourselves do we show to others?

Process

Consider the masks you or those around you might wear.

1. This can be literal masks like in sports or Halloween.
2. This can be figurative masks like the role you play as a sibling, daughter, son, friend, musician, athlete. What is expected of you in these roles? What feels comfortable to you? What feels like a lot of work, or even stressful?
3. This can be a different kind of mask, maybe the decisions you make about clothing, hairstyle, style, make-up -- and the reasons you make these choices.

Using a format of your choosing, write a poem about a mask or masks. I went with a free verse poem, but maybe a Golden Shovel is more to your liking today.

Mentor Poem

"Inherited Mask" by Mo Daley

I inherited this mask from my mother,
who I believe, inherited hers from her mother.
How many generations have veiled themselves
in masks of stoicism and calm?
In masks of patience and understanding?
We are strong women, by all accounts,
revered for our ability to deftly handle the most extreme
circumstances.

But it is onerous,
living life hiding behind a mask
trying not to let the plaster crack,
fulfilling expectations that have been thrust upon me,
only displaying my veneer to the world.

Vulnerability may be an option,
but how can an old woman
unyoke an inherited mask?

15. When I Grow Up
The original prompt is from Angie Braatan

Inspiration

Angie highly recommends Chen Chen's "When I Grow Up I Want to Be a List of Further Possibilities" and then his whole poetry book by the same name. After reading the poem, she immediately thought about all the things that she wanted to be and wished to be, if not confined to such a limited life. (Imagine how fun it would be to write to this prompt at different ages of one's life, and compare your reflections - we hope you will always keep a poetry notebook and pursue this idea.)

Process

- Think about everything you want to be if you could be anything in the world.
- Make it funny or honest or a mixture of the two.
- Add in some detail and metaphor, as Chen Chen does.
- Your choice: Any form is possible today

Mentor Poem

"When I Grow Up I Want to Be Other Things" by Angie Braatan

To be everything that I wanted to be but did not choose to be, like Sylvia in her fig tree, I want to be able to choose everything and not sit withering away
Like a full time writer and successful
Like a PE teacher, active, to be my own energy and other people's also
To be a personal assistant because I don't really care to tell people what to do but if you give me a list of things that need to be done, they'll be done before this poem is over
To be a more patient caretaker for my grandma
To be a mom, earlier in life, knowing by now what kind of ten year old child I would have
To be a nicer person
To be a more lovable person
To be a more talkative person
To be a more outgoing person
who feeds off of conversation instead of hiding from it
To be the love my mother needs
To be the love my brother needs
To be the judge who decides my niece and nephew will not be taken away from their father
To be the judge who decides that _ should be convicted for killing _ (insert too many names into the blanks)
To be some spirit who doesn't allow these things to happen in the first place
To be some non-prejudiced oxygen that flows into the lungs and ends up in the heart of otherwise racist people so they don't kill anyone because of skin color or who they pray to, or where they were born, or, or, or
To be everything that is fair and good.

References

Berryhill, A. (2023, April 15). What you missed. Ethical ELA. https://www.ethicalela.com/what-you-missed/

Braatan, A. (2023, July 21). When I grow up. Ethical ELA. https://www.ethicalela.com/when-i-grow-up/

Crandall, B.R. (2022, April 5). Poetic drive-by. Ethical ELA. https://www.ethicalela.com/poetic-drive-bys/

Daley, M. (2023, July 15) Masks we wear. Ethical ELA. https://www.ethicalela.com/the-masks-we-wear/

Daley, M. (2024, April 8). Zip code poem. Ethical ELA. https://www.ethicalela.com/zip-code-poem/

Donovan, S. (2022, April 20). I sing, writer. Ethical ELA. https://www.ethicalela.com/13614/

Johnson, K. (2022, April 11). Quirky poems. Ethical ELA. https://www.ethicalela.com/quirky-poems/

Mitchel, L. (2022, April 25). Scientific method. Ethical ELA. https://www.ethicalela.com/scientific-method/

Opager, J. (2021, April 25). Perspective poem. Ethical ELA. https://www.ethicalela.com/perspective-poem

Pitre, L. (2022, April 21). When you need a break. Ethical ELA. https://www.ethicalela.com/when-you-need-a-break-go-to-a-place-of-comfort/

Schoenborn, A. (2022, April 14). Tumble down poetry. Ethical ELA. https://www.ethicalela.com/tumble-down-poetry/

Vasinda, S. (2022, April 19). How to be. Ethical ELA. https://www.ethicalela.com/how-to-be/

Wiley, J. (2023, June 17). What about your friends. Ethical ELA. https://www.ethicalela.com/what-about-your-friends/

Chapter 4: Extending Our Community

Dear Teacher,

When the calendar flips to November and December, what comes to mind? Suffice to say - these two months are filled with high expectations. There are many rituals and traditions, including celebrations and holidays with family and friends, special concerts, theater shows, and sports tournaments. All this fanfare means holiday interruptions, vacations, absences. There is often joy and stress in welcoming others and/or being a guest. Our daily schedules are out of whack, routines are broken, and we move through a fog of late nights, heavy food, and less sleep.

It can also be a time filled with reflection - who are the important people in our lives, how do we give to others, what are we hoping to receive? For some of us, these are not days of joy, but times when we feel sadness, grief, and pain. Perhaps we are responding to discomfort with 'forced' family-social situations or anxious about family holidays spent with blended or divorced families. Maybe we feel lonely, or are spending too much time away from friends, or we are home alone, taking care of siblings.

November and December can be a great time to think about others and their needs, a time to welcome a larger community. Consider physically walking the neighborhood, connecting with others in school, and letting them know they matter. This is a great time of year to start new traditions in your school - new ways to make and share food together, and/or bringing in local community arts and experiences, perhaps even poetry readings with peers.

117

Teachers and students - you know yourself best, you know what you are experiencing right now. Be alert to your level of fatigue and practice good self-care during all of this. In this season of change, allow yourself to write incomplete poems, rough fragments - use this ritual of poetry writing time to center and surface excitements and anxieties, use this time as release.

We offer a sequence of poems, but feel free to go in any order that works for you and your students.

Peace,
Sarah, Mo, & Maureen

*Just a gentle reminder to check out the resources on
www.ethicala.com for additional support.
Sending comfort your way.*

1. Día de los Muertos
Original prompt by Anna J. Small Roseboro

Inspiration

In early November, *Día de los Muertos* is celebrated throughout Mexico and by people of Latinx heritage elsewhere. It is a joyous occasion where people reflect on the lives of those who have died. Creating an *ofrenda* ("offering" in Spanish) is an essential part of the celebration. These are also called *altares* or *alters*, but they are not for worship. Rather, *ofrendas* are set up to remember and honor the memory of an ancestor. *Ofrendas* include the four elements (water, wind, earth, and fire) in addition to a photo of the person to whom the altar is dedicated and things that person enjoyed in life.

Process

Write an *ofrenda* poem (an elegy, an ode) about someone you love who you have lost. Write about what your person enjoyed in life. Alternatively, think of someone of Latinx heritage who made a valuable contribution and write a poem of celebration about them. For both approaches, make a list of what is special about this person, and let these form the basis of your poem today. Suggestion - Try a quatrain (four lines) in iambic pentameter (or about 10 syllables each). Any form is welcome as is any length. Whatever time and energy permits.

Mentor Poem

"Elegy to Arturo Alphonzo Schomburg, Archiver of History" by Anna J. Small Roseboro

They told him his folks had no history.
He spent years proving them wrong.
He collected books and art and letters
Proving contributions to culture and song.

He immigrated to the USA and joined the band.
Not as a musician, but as an archiving man.
During the years of Harlem Renaissance
This Afro Puerto Rican man took a stand.
Schomberg joined intellectuals there.
They had done so much and had much to say
About their participation in progress of this nation.
Inventors and educators, skilled in business and science
Records collected and preserved for all who would question.

Because of his passion and knowledge
He was successful working at Fisk College.
He used what he learned, misinformation he spurned
With the library he built those rumors he kil't.
And now you can visit yourself.
Check the art on the wall and books on the shelf.

2. Rituals & Traditions
Original prompt by Susie Morice

Inspiration
We generally all gravitate toward certain rituals or routine acts that seem to have a sort of comforting rhythm, a familiarity. Often these involve traditional details and props that help smooth the edges of the moment. Our daily lives are full of universals: those "aha" types of "yes, that's something I do, we all do," those resonant acts that take us through a moment. It might be as simple as bathing in a tub – we swish the water from side to side, distributing the water temperature till it feels just right and we can lower ourselves entirely into the tub. It might be that moment at home plate as we screw our bodies into that stance and haul the bat up and in ready position for a swing as we connect our eyes to the ball in the pitcher's hand. It might also be an almost ceremonial act, wherein you play an expected role in an expected environment, following the protocols passed down from generation to generation. This prompt may find both the ritual that rings familiar yet also puts you uniquely in the middle, making this both typical or familiar as well as unique to you and your perspective.

Process
- List 3-4 rituals/routines/traditional acts in your day, in your life things in which you are an active participant.
- Find a listening ear and talk with that person about 2 of those rituals/traditions. Let that person discuss his or her rituals/routines that percolate up into the discourse. (I am a firm believer that discourse prior to writing is a powerful prewriting act.)
- Settle on one ritual/traditional moment that seems to take the lead in your heart and mind.
- Make a list of as many words and phrases that come to mind as you can, recounting all the "stuff" that is present during this moment – concrete things that help this moment take shape.
- Add colors and sounds that are part of recreating that moment.
- Have fun with this. Your poem might unearth a comforting scene. On the other hand, it may expose a tradition that needs to break its hold.

Mentor Poem

"It seems kind of silly" by Mo Daley

It seems kind of silly when I think about it
but, it's MY ritual, and I like it.
In fact, I may need it.
I get up with the dogs long before the sun peeks above the
horizon.
They wander the yard for a few minutes regardless of the
weather
checking to see who has visited us during the night.
I put on my tea water and fill a bowl with yogurt or cereal,
whatever is around. It really isn't that important.
The dogs race through the door as they hear me prepare
their food.
They eat.
I eat.
My tea steeps.

3. Storytime Poems
Original prompt by Kim Johnson

Inspiration

Stories are the fabric of who we are. Stories are how we are raised, how we learn, and how we are entertained. Our best times are often spent listening to the stories of others.

Process

Think of the stories – and storytellers – in your life. These may be family matriarchs or patriarchs, other family members, friends, or perhaps even professionals at storytelling festivals and podcasts such as The Moth. Write a poem about a storyteller or a story that has had an impact on you.

Mentor Poem

"Family Dinner" by Kim Johnson

His greatest stories never started with words.
They began at his heart.
He patted down his shirt pocket
fumbled for his pen
furrowed his wild and unkempt eyebrows
slid his coffee and half-eaten pie to the edge of the table
flattened his napkin and ironed out the creases with the
side of his wrinkled hand
clicked his pen
sketched a Parkinson's- jagged diagram
grasped the bottom of an imaginary globe
drew in a raspy, phlegm-filled breath
and held his audience captive.
He still does.
[This prompt might be awesome to repeat in January -
sharing about something that 'went down' over winter
break?]

4. House in the Sky
Original prompt by Darius Phelps

Inspiration

Darius draws inspiration from the poet Kyle Liang's book *How to Build A House.* In old Chinese tradition, families would burn houses filled with furniture because it was believed that it would then be waiting for them in the afterlife. Today we will imagine our poetry as 'a burning house,' an offering for everafter.

Process

For today's poem, think of a person or object as the direct address and include what they or it needs most, which is what the speaker of the poem will burn for them. Another approach is for the speaker to be the person or object writing to you as the subject. What do you need? What is waiting for you?

Mentor Poem

"House in the Sky *after Kyle Liang*" by Darius Phelps

Mother do not worry
I'll burn you a house in the sky
One where you finally learn to love yourself
So you can love me the way that I've needed since the day his
infidelity stole your soul
Each brick laid with intent,
I'll make sure this time, he can't come in.
I'll make it one fit for a queen,
one where you'll finally learn
how to spread your wings
One where our demons
won't determine and deteriorate our bond
But instead we walk hand in hand,
just like we used to
No more false gods and failed prayers
No more wondering, if he's really there.
One where I'll return to being your little man
And not the man.
Only he knows how many tears I've cried
This house in the sky will set you free
Even if it takes every little piece that's left of me.

5. Thanks
Original prompt offered by Sarah J. Donovan

Inspiration

Much obliged. Appreciation. Gratitude. Acknowledgment. Recognition. Blessing. Grace. Praise. Perhaps your days and nights are filled with incessant to-do lists and projects. Perhaps you find yourself non-stop scrolling. Perhaps you are trying to keep yourself from feeling whatever is out there waiting — something like grief, or it could be fear, maybe it's apathy, or it could even just be: you. If you are feeling out of sorts, poetry is there for you, a welcome respite. To heal, to avoid — it doesn't matter how or why we are using this poetry space. There is no judgment here. What matters is that you are here. Yes, that you are here. Let's find our synonym for *thanks* that *we* are here.

Process

Reflect on the words of thanks to name the space you want to be in with your writing today.

- Has a person changed your life for the better? If so, recognize who and why?
- Describe a friendship that has been a blessing. When, how, why?
- Can you find a moment when someone made a difference? Describe the situation, bring us into the interaction. Was it a "much obliged" or "appreciation"?
- What about you/ your being has kept you going these months? Can you recognize that in you?
- Do you need to give yourself grace? What would you say or do for yourself to offer grace?
- If you would like some distance from the "I," maybe you can name some thanks you witnessed in the world, in your home, between strangers, even between pets. Show us that blessing, grace, and acknowledgment in your verse today.

For the form, look at Joseph Bruchac's poem, "Prints." Source: *Sing: Poetry from the Indigenous Americas* (University of Arizona Press, 2011).

Mentor Poem

"recognition" by Sarah J. Donovan

seeing your wavy hair
with gray strands kissing
the part, a line laying
bare our path back
is like looking
into the mirror
I've shrouded in
distance, distraction
that holds
our childhood–
distortions uncurve
in the iris of your eyes
disfigures unbend
in the teared cheeks
I see
with a sister's eye
the was in my am
the was in your is
and the healing
that remains
for us

6. Twenty Questions
Original prompt by Allison Berryhill

Inspiration

Jim Moore's "Twenty Questions" is ultimately about the choices we make in our lives and the lingering doubt that underpins those choices. Its opening line beckons you to look at the sky, and concludes with the haunting question: Did I already ask that?

Process

The invitation is for you to write a question, then another, and follow it through memory and imagery until you have (maybe) twenty questions. Consider the choices that have made a difference in your life. Maybe end your poem with "Did I already ask that?"

Mentor Poem

"Twenty Questions From My Classroom" by Allison Berryhill

Why am I here?
In this chair, by this desk?
Am I flinging finite minutes?
of my life into the dusty swirl of students' too-full thoughts?
Are my words rolling tumbleweeds skirting across this barren plain?
Where is your hall pass?
Why am I wasting breath, breath, breath?
Will another Wednesday roll out from under me in 33-minute sprints?
What do they ask:
What did I miss yesterday?
Why are we reading this?
Where's Corbin Logeman?
And why do we say "have run" and not "have ran"?
Does it make a difference?
And to who?
Or to whom?
What is the color of teal?
Where is the receipt book?
Can I go to the nurse?
Do they learn anything?
Did I already ask that?

7. Feelings
Original inspiration offered by Melanie Crowder

Inspiration

We are living through turbulent times — there's an understatement for you! Thankfully, poetry is one of the most illuminating and cathartic ways to put that experience down on the page. Let's refresh and refocus through poetry.

Process

Identify the emotional state you want to express and write it down at the top of your paper. Brainstorm things in the physical world around you that are illustrative of that inner state. Nature offers inspiration, but mechanical or industrial objects would be fascinating as well. Write a first draft freely, without mentioning your emotions or the circumstances prompting the poem. Let the image you create through your words stand on its own. Sift through the words on the page, say them out loud, think about sounds that convey or mimic your emotional state. Trim your words down to only the most essential, until the texture of your poem paints as distinct a picture as the image.

Mentor Poem

"Deep Inside" by Melanie Crowder

Deep inside,
the longleaf pine
turns water and sunlight
into turpentine.
Deep down,
the longleaf pine
craves fire.
Every few years,
the forest grows thick
with leaf litter and split trees,
needles scattered
like matchsticks.
Can you hear the crackle beneath your step?
Can you taste the resin and smoke
on your tongue?
The air is ripe with it.
The forest longs
to burn.

8. Disrupting Thanksgiving
Original prompt by Sarah J. Donovan

Inspiration

Today, open up your poetry notebook and revisit the poetry prompts to date. Is there an inspiration that speaks to you? Create a new poem in response.

As an alternative and in the spirit of naming harm and cultivating healing, you are invited to spend some time before Thanksgiving break disrupting the myths of the first Thanksgiving.

Process

Judy Dow (Abenaki) writes, "What is it about the story of "The First Thanksgiving" that makes it essential to be taught in virtually every grade from preschool through high school? What is it about the story that is so seductive? Why has it become an annual elementary school tradition to hold Thanksgiving pageants, with young children dressing up in paper-bag costumes and feather-duster headdresses and marching around the schoolyard?" She goes on to offer eleven (11) myths and facts about Thanksgiving here. Choose one myth, and write a poem that names the harm and, in the spirit of healing, illuminates the fact. Write either a nonet or a diamante.

You could also read any of these articles by Sarah's children's literature mentor Debbie Reese and craft a poem based on what you learned or want others to know:

- Native Stories: Books for tweens and teens by and about Indigenous peoples, by Kara Stewart and Debbie Reese, at *School Library Journal* on August 20, 2019.
- "We Are Still Here": An Interview with Debbie Reese in *English Journal,* in 2016.
- Critical Indigenous Literacies: Selecting and Using Children's Books about Indigenous Peoples, by Debbie Reese in Volume 92, Number 6 of *Language Arts* (published in 2018).
- Twelve Picture Books that Showcase Native Voices by Debbie Reese in *School Library Journal* in 2018.

Mentor Poem

"Our Roots" by Sarah J. Donovan

This poem is a "found poem," using language from Judy
Dow's article to shape this nonet.

A deep need to believe our roots are
not soiled by guilt. If we dare turn
the dirt, sowed violations
bloom truths untold. Excise
myths, rip falsity
from prose & verse
so truth-seeds
flourish
heal.

9. Gifted Words
Original prompt by Jennifer Guyor Jowett

Inspiration

Writers gift us with words. They willingly give of themselves, and while their hope for our love of the gift is nestled deep in every line, they expect nothing in return. Their titles give hint to what is inside, like wrapping: prettied up or pulled together sparingly. During this season of giving, we can turn to the words already shared with us, to the gift writers have placed into our hands, and gift them back by repackaging them.

Process

Create a poem with words from a fellow poet, their gift to you. Read through your notes from poetry read-alouds - what lines of others resonated for you? Browse the poetry wall of your classroom, reading words of your classmates. Jot down words or phrases or themes that jump out at you. Perhaps focus on the poetry title only, and weave the title into a line of your poem. Create a new poem of your own, with these words at the heart. Bonus challenge: consider writing a Fibonacci poem, where the number of syllables in each line of the poem is the sum of the previous two lines, 1, 1, 2, 3, 5, 8. Have fun!

Mentor Poem

"Please" by Maureen Young Ingram

~Fibonacci poem, using words from yesterday's nonet by
Dr. Sarah J. Donovan

Please
know
this truth
about me
I'm not soiled by guilt
I'm fertilized by fearful love

10. Abuelito Who
Original prompt by Stacey L. Joy

Inspiration

This time of holidays and celebration never fails to stir up memories of those who are absent or no longer with us. With this poem, we invite you to put some of these reflections into poetry.

Process

Separate a page into 5 sections or columns for your five senses. Make a sensory chart of memories, descriptions, details, and emotions as you think about a lost loved one, pet, or even a "no longer loving you" loved one
.

Consider the smallest or least obvious details to bring into your poem. If figurative language, rhymes, or imagery will enhance your poem, go for it.

Read *Abuelito Who* **by Sandra Cisneros** for inspiration. There is no required format, but try using "Who" where it fits, and consider using only one punctuation at the beginning or the end. You may title it "_____Who..." or whatever you choose.

Mentor Poem

"Daddy Who" by Seana Hurd Wright

Daddy, who taught me to ride a bike in an Inglewood
alley
who fed me oatmeal, Cheerios, and rice for breakfast
who fostered my addiction to television shows
who loved Sanford and Son and Bob Hope movies
Daddy who eventually left Mommy and moved nearby
thanks for dropping by and leaving money for me
sometimes
thanks for reminding me that you still loved me
thanks for mostly supporting me through college
but didn't attend my graduation due to his fear of planes
Daddy who lovingly walked me down the aisle
Daddy who PESTERED me about becoming a teacher
like he and Mommy were
it's in your DNA he would say
he always gave my daughters savings bonds
and told them to attend college
Daddy who called to tell me about the tumor
who fought for three years to stay here
Daddy who is gone now
Daddy whose eyes are mine
I see your love daily

11. I Remember
Original prompt by Kim Johnson

Inspiration

In *The Last Avant-Garde: The Making of the New York School of Poets* by David Lehman, readers learn that Joe Brainard went to spend the summer of 1969 in Vermont, where he began writing short anaphoristic snippets of memories, all beginning with the words, "I Remember," thus defining a new poetic form.

Process

- *Reminisce*: This can be a time and place in your life that you want to revisit, that will bring you joy or comfort in these unprecedented times.
- *Ponder! Unearth! Ruminate!* Or this can be a time and place in your life that you want to re-imagine with new eyes and perspective. Maybe you will write this from another's point of view.
- *Imagine*: Spring into the future and imagine what you will or want to remember. Or go for fiction — write something sci-fi, fantasy, or fairytale-ish.

Your poem can be as short or as long as you need it to be today. Give yourself permission for "good enough." And give yourself permission to reject this idea altogether and write whatever you need today.

Mentor Poem

"I Remember" by Kim Johnson

I remember clutching her warm hand as the death rattle
beat the drum of her final march
deferring to my brother, "I picked the spot. You pick the
plot"
I remember pleading, "Lord, I need a sign she can rest in
peace"
confessing I'd prayed for a sign: a majestic bird in flight,
wings outstretched, assuring peace
I remember fighting tears, wanting to shoot three birds
circling overhead
resisting the urge to punch my brother, who was fighting
his own tears......of laughter?
I remember eyeing him, raising one questioning brow,
tightening my lips, muttering obscenities
wondering if he was drunk as he whispered sideways,
"She showed up! With her parents!"
I remember feeling the full force of her humor, her sign:
sending buzzards in place of an eagle
I remember my animal-loving mother – prankish and
ever-present. Even now.

12. Giving
Original prompt by Sarah J. Donovan

Inspiration

Take some time to reflect on what exists today because of you. Give yourself some grace to think about what is good because of you. What exists, what endures, what lives, what thrives because you have given of yourself, your time, your being, your wisdom, your body?

Process

To begin, make a list. Open your notebook and take inventory:

- places that you have created
- beings you have created, nurtured
- objects, artifacts you have imagined, invented, passed along
- meals you have made, recipes you have shared
- habits of heart, of mind that you have loved into existence
- stories, poems that exist because you listened or asked for them
- experiences you have offered, invited, organized

Then, see if that inventory might be a poem in itself or, perhaps, you are drawn to explore one in a longer poem or several in a series of stanzas.

Mentor Poem

"How to Make a Poem Become" by Sarah J. Donovan

How to make a poem become
is different for everyone. The first
word may
ignite imagery
and metaphor or
be erased in backspace
only to return in the
last line alongside a
collective pronoun,
parentheses, or
empty space.
From that word,
the poem becomes
a great Elm
refusing to bend in
an ice storm;
a firefly
lighting up a dance party
for one.
The poem
becomes a swing
moving harm to
healing;
a tea kettle
firing
up the whistle to
warm hardened
hearts.
But how to make a poem become
no one can say. It starts way
before the blank page
when the brain and heart
relay to waiting digits or tongue
that first word to
become
a
poem.

13. Conversations
Original prompt by Susie Morice

Inspiration

Nature offers us meaningful conversations. So often we buzz past and through the huge slices of nature that are all around us as if they were just stage scenery for Beckett's Godot, rather than our experiencing the intricate, enormous, endless, breathing, living environments that we take for granted. The tree when we look closely bends to reach out and capture rays, muscling its way through the crowd to rise above the din of humanity at its feet. Just listening in can be transcending. (Suggestion, read - *"Sparrow, What Did You Say?"* Ada Limon, Poet Laureate)

Process

Take yourself to nature…think back to a moment when you stood quiet in the grace of Nature, or grab a coat/jacket/sweater and walk outside to stand in your own tiny piece. Were you to have a conversation, as you stand there, who is listening? What questions might you ask? Conversations are ways we connect, ways we find common ground, ways we sort out our thinking, ways we thread ourselves together, ways we lean into each other. Perhaps make this poem a conversation with that entity in nature.

Mentor Poem

"Were I to translate the trees" by Glenda Funk

Were I to translate the trees'
Whispers through rustling leaves,
I wonder if they would weep like
The Willow by a pond,
Her fingers cascading into
Glassy water, breaking its surface the
Way democracy cracked
On the sixth day of a new year.
I hear earth's cries, her muted,
Wailing absorbed into inky stars
Light years away, safe from
Insurrection and the dispossessed.
Through Aspen branches
Reaching heavenward
Nature claws its way to safe space
Not of this world but in it.
She bears witness to truths,
Our world translatable and broken.

14. Horatian Ode
Original prompt by Mo Daley and Tracie McCormick

Inspiration

An ode is used to celebrate someone or something, and there are many types. The ode form we propose is that of the Latin lyric poet Horace. His style is a bit less structured and more <u>intimate</u> and reflective. The Horatian ode creates a calm and contemplative tone, meant to bring peace. Horatian odes have more than one stanza, usually between three and five, and all of the stanzas follow the same rhyme structure and meter.

Process

What does our generation do when we want to celebrate someone or something? We tell the world about it by posting it on social media, of course! Scroll through your feeds. What jumps out at you? Choose a subject that excites you. Is there a person, place, thing, or event that you think is just wonderful (or conversely, that you hate?) and about which you have many things to say? Think about how your subject makes you feel and jot down some adjectives. What makes it special or unique? What is your personal connection to the subject? How has the subject impacted you? What are some descriptive words you can use? What are some specific qualities of your subject?

Mentor Poem

"Ode to Mr. Rogers" by Tracie McCormack

Mr. Rogers, you saw our youth as more than just kids
who should remain seen and not heard.
You encouraged them to speak
while you listened and learned.
Mr. Rogers, you saw our diversity as more than just traits
that shame and divide.
You encouraged us to celebrate
while you showcased them with pride.
Mr. Rogers, you saw our disasters as more than just causes
of trauma.
You encouraged helpers
to foster benevolent karma.
Mr. Rogers, you saw our feelings as more than just
weakness
requiring suppression.
You encouraged us to face them
through appropriate expression.
Mr. Rogers, you saw civic contributions as more than just
a dreaded responsibility.
You encouraged us to serve others
making this a place we want to be.

15. An Ode to the Unworthy
Original prompt by Jordan Stamper

Inspiration

When Jordan taught Pre-AP English II to 10th graders in Houston, TX, she taught a unit on "The Purpose of Poetry." Students explored various forms of poetry with the intention of praising, mocking, or mourning their subjects. Within her reading and preparing for the unit, she stumbled upon Elizabeth Acevedo's "Rat Ode." The inspiration behind the poem was all too familiar to her. A writing professor Acevedo had deemed rats as "not noble enough" for a poem. As we, and our students, learn to claim the label of "writer," those who come before us, even our teachers, are our inspiration. But what happens when a subject, a genre, a form, is deemed not worthy?

Process

In the spirit of extending our community, look around your space, neighborhood, city and look for objects often overlooked or perhaps deemed not worthy of a poem. Write an ode for them. An ode tends to praise or glorify its subject with flowery language and a slightly formal tone. Odes are also a great vehicle for practicing various forms of sensory language. Using Acevedo's "Rat Ode' as inspiration, write the following:
- Pick a subject that many would not think worthy of a poem.
- Brainstorm your sensory language. What does the subject look/feel/sound/smell/taste like?
- Choose the sensory language that could be written in praise of this subject.
- Write an ode to your subject incorporating the sensory language. Odes come in all forms, so you are not limited to rhyme scheme, meter, length, etc.

Mentor Poem

"Ode to a Vulture" by Jordan Stamper

Your talons scrape asphalt in front of my car,
Sleek black wings spanned out rival that of eagles'.
Your bladed beak snatches remnants of tendon
And muscle tenderized by tires. Tirelessly,
Your committees clean roads, ditches,
Partake in bloated bodies collapsed in fields.
If only you had more recognition for staving off
Disease or the infestation of maggots and flies.
The crown of red feathers nods to my bumper,
But oh king of this marsh, we bow to you.

References

Berryhill, A. (2020, February 15.). February, day 1/5 : Twenty questions Ethical ELA. https://www.ethicalela.com/february-day-1-5-twenty-questions-poems/

Berryhill, A. (2020, February 17). February day 3/5: apology poem. Ethical ELA. https://www.ethicalela.com/february-day-3-5-apology-poem/

Crowder, M. (2020, June 24). June #openwrite: Writing with author Melanie Crowder. Ethical ELA. https://www.ethicalela.com/june-openwrite-writing-with-author-melanie-crowder/

Daley, M., & McCormick, T. (2020, July 19). July #openwrite: ode. Ethical ELA. https://www.ethicalela.com/july-openwrite-ode/

Donovan, S. (2020, November 14). thanks. Ethical ELA. https://www.ethicalela.com/thanks/

Donovan, S. (2020, November 15). giving. Ethical ELA. https://www.ethicalela.com/giving/

Donovan, S. (2020, November 18). heal. Ethical ELA. https://www.ethicalela.com/heal/

Johnson, K. (2019, July 19). July 5/5 - day writing challenge. Ethical ELA. https://www.ethicalela.com/july-5-5-day-writing-challenge/

Johnson, K. (2020, May 16). May #openwrite: "I remember". Ethical ELA. https://www.ethicalela.com/may-1-5-i-remember-openwrite/

Joy, S. L. (2020, January 18). Day 1, Abuelito who: January writing challenge. Ethical ELA.

https://www.ethicalela.com/day-1-abuelito-who-january-writing-challenge/

Morice, S. (2019, November 10). November 1/5 - day writing challenge. Ethical ELA. https://www.ethicalela.com/november-1-5-day-writing-challenge/

Morice, S. (2021, January 16). Conversations. Ethical ELA. https://www.ethicalela.com/conversations/

Phelps, D. (2023, April 21). House in the sky. Ethical ELA. https://www.ethicalela.com/house-in-the-sky/

Roseboro, A.J.S. {2019, September 18)). Día de los muertos. Ethical ELA. https://www.ethicalela.com/september-5-5-day-challenge/

Resources

Lehman, D. *The Last Avant-Garde: The Making of the New York School of Poets* . (1999: Anchor).

Liang, K. *How to Build A House*. (2018: Swan Scythe Press). ISBN 978-1-930454-46-0. 39 pps.

Limon, A. *"Sparrow, Sparrow, What Did You Say?" The Carrying*.

Moore, J. "Twenty Questions." https://poets.org/poem/twenty-questions

Williams, C. W. *"This Is Just To Say"* https://www.poetryfoundation.org/poems/56159/this-is-just-to-say

Chapter 5: Healing Ways

Dear Teacher,

All teachers learn very quickly to expect the unexpected.
The best-laid plans will come undone for sundry reasons.
It might be something as natural as an unexpected winter
storm that closes the school and breaks up the continuity
of day-to-day studies. Perhaps you have only half your
students on a given day, or your class period has been
reduced to a fragment of its usual allotted time, or your
marking period ends on a Thursday and you are left
wondering what to do with that dangling Friday.

There are many 'outside the classroom' situations that can
affect both students and teachers alike. Days when
something unforeseen shakes you and your students to
their core. It can be challenging to go on with planned
lessons in the midst of disturbing local or world events, or
the personal suffering of a student, family, or faculty
member.

Use this section of the book during those surprising times
of transition, when you are not sure what exactly you
need beyond the assurance that poetry will help. These
poetry prompts are meant to meet you where you are at -
yes, while things are in upheaval. One might call these
healing prompts, a way to catch one's breath by playing
with words. This daily poetry practice offers the choice to
process or escape, an opportunity to buffer oneself from
the uncertainty and anxiety of the world that surrounds.

This section offers both space and embrace for your poetry
community. As their teacher, you are aware of individual
loads that students are carrying at any given time. Is it

best to write poetry that allows students to delve deeper into the ache that is most on their mind right now? Or is it better to use poetry as a meditative device, allowing students to let go of worries and pressures by taking their writing to a whole other place? We are often distracted by a writing puzzle or a specific syllable count, and in this way, such prompts can be healing. Only you know what your students need most.

A reminder - treat all writers with dignity. In times of transition and upheaval, it is all the more important to allow your students the privacy of writing; let them share if they desire.

We are instilling a life-long love for writing poetry.

Peace,
Sarah, Mo, & Maureen

1. Grammatically Ungrammatical
Original prompt by Jennifer Guyor Jowett

Inspiration

A writing conversation with a student-led to Jennifer wondering what might happen if grammatical rules suddenly didn't apply. Students and teacher tossed ideas around. We already verbify nouns, but what if nouns were verbs? What if colors described verbs, and adverbs modified nouns? Poetry begs for rules to be broken. As Jennifer and her class mulled the possibilities of breaking grammar rules in poetry, they were inspired by the poem "River" by Sherwin Bitsui, a Dine´ of the Navajo Reservation in Arizona, which begins, "When we river" - using a noun as a verb. (Feel free to look up this poem as your own inspiration.)

Process

Play with grammar. Change nouns to verbs. Change verbs to nouns. Use adjectives to describe verbs. You might begin with Bitsui's line "When we… and add a noun. Jennifer found it worked to start with a couple of ungrammatical lines and add a few lines to ground the reader before playing more. Turn the rules on their heads. It's ok. Really.

Mentor Poem

"When we highway" by Jennifer Guyor Jowett

When we highway
between birth and end,
our yellow moving,
blue moving, red moving,
our days minutes
our weeks days
in constant motion,
month upon month
as years grow and pass,
a black crow in the fields of corn,
blinking our reflection,
there and gone,
heads a tilt,
wonders what he saw

2. Right Words at the Right Time
Original prompt offered by Kim Johnson on May 20, 2020

Inspiration

Has anyone ever said anything prophetic to you? Words that impacted your future? These words might come as guidance from someone you know well, perhaps in a conversation that is specifically tailored to this very topic - discussing your future. Or, perhaps even more often, prescient words are said without much fanfare, woven into an ordinary conversation, and a phrase or a feeling settles in your mind. You reflect upon these words from time to time, and then, something occurs that makes you think - "Ah! That's exactly like what was said to me, what we were talking about."

Process

Consider the people whose words were your guiding lights in direction and decision-making. How did they help you make an important decision or to see things from a more clarifying perspective?

Mentor Poem

"She told me many months later" by Mo Daley

She told me many months later
how she knew I was her friend.
She could trace it back to one moment in time.
I was dumbfounded.
What could she possibly mean?
She spoke of her weariness
when her mother-in-law died-
the countless hours on her feet at the wake,
the need to be the face of the family at such a trying time.
She told me how happy she was to see me at the funeral
home.
She appreciated the condolence call from a coworker.
But then she said, "You took your coat off.
In that moment, I knew you were there for me as a
friend."
An inconsequential act on my part
meant the world to her in her hour of need.
I had no idea at the time.
Now whenever I can I tell people to take their coats off.

3. Come, Join My Reality
Original prompt by Amber Harrison

Inspiration

Abstract words refer to thoughts or feelings: love, grief, hope, life, or death. Concrete words are tangible: things we can experience through our senses of touch, taste, sight, smell, and sound. We can bring others into our reality when we share our abstract thoughts and feelings in a concrete way.

Process

Pick an object within reach of where you are right now. What emotion does this object bring to you? Use the abstract word as your poem title, but use only concrete words in your poem to bring your readers into your reality, being sure to identify the different senses related to this emotion and object.

Mentor Poem

"Still Hangry" by Amber Harrison

Before I went to sleep last night
I filled and whisked a wide-mouth mason Ball jar:
> half a cup of oats and almond mile,
> a tablespoon of chia seeds and powdered peanut
butter
> plus a dash of warm woodsy spice--ground
cinnamon.

At work today---
> grumbling tummy,
> blurred vision,
> slow and heavy steps---
I pop the lid of that mason jar.
My white, plastic spoon swirls the mix.

First bite---
> my shoulders drop
> my eyes roll to the sky.
I forgot a tablespoon of Pure Vermont maple syrup.
Bleh!

4. What a Wonderful World
Original prompt by Stacey L. Joy

Inspiration

Stacey loves delicious and soothing words, savoring words that name those things that are sometimes indescribable. For this prompt, we'll be inspired by beautiful, delectable words. Perhaps the word will help you share something you have been holding in a safe secret place. Perhaps the word will inspire you to unpack or view something from a new perspective. You might even find a word that helps you better understand something from the past, present or future. *Note to poets*: start a 'wonderful words' collection in your notebooks. As you read, hear, and discover new words, list them and their meanings in the back of your poetry notebook.

Process

Choose a word or a few words that resonate with you. There are fun word lists available on the internet, such as Berlitz.com, which offers a rabbit hole of unique and beautiful words.

What word calls out to you? Why? Jot down some ideas that come to your heart and mind.

Suggestion: Try writing a Haiku Sonnet: 4 haiku and two lines at the end to make a total of 14 lines like a sonnet.

Mentor Poem

"Ubuntu" by Stacey L. Joy

(a Haiku Sonnet)
Ubuntu
Our joy is a gift
Ancestors' prayers and dreams
Came to pass for us
Our love, enduring
Generations prevailing
Rising together
Our hopes for the world
Safe spaces to live and learn
Fearless, audacious
Our strength is mighty
Gives meaning to Ubuntu
Powered to push on
I am, we are, each others'
Healing redemption song

5. Re-Encounters
Original prompt by Shaun Ingalls

Inspiration

Poetry is relationship. We can't help but draw inspiration from other poets, we write and build on what came before, our words breathe into those of others, and so the circle grows. Poetry invites us to reflect, to look back. When we read our own words or those of other poets, we hear something new. Our perspective changes with the passage of time and we see things differently.

Process

Take another look at something, anything. Maybe you are reflecting on an earlier situation or circumstances. Perhaps you are rethinking beliefs or assumptions. You might even revisit something as basic as a chore you performed.

This is also a good opportunity to review one of your earlier poems. Has your perspective changed? Do you feel differently now? Re-encounter this earlier part of you and let it inspire your writing today. *Note*: If you choose to revisit an earlier poem, consider drawing a strikeout line through words that no longer ring true for you, with your new perspective following these strikeouts. For inspiration, feel free to look up the poem "Drift" by Alicia Mountain.

Mentor Poem

"seasons together" by Maureen Young Ingram

spring is the dogwood's
creamy white flowers
with a kiss of pink
canopied by the great tree's
yellow-green embrace

a bird or breeze carried
the dogwood's seed
to my backyard
so many years ago
a chance encounter

the tall maple adored
this gift from above
offering hard roots
within which to nestle
sheltering the seedling

together
slowly steadily
they have grown
season upon season
alongside one another

ever
lasting
until

6. What Have You Lost?
Original prompt by Allison Berryhill

Inspiration

What have you lost? In all probability, you've lost little things–that favorite hairbrush, a ticket to the spaghetti supper–as well as things that have left holes in your heart: that journal from high school, an opportunity, a loved one.

Process

Take a few minutes to make a list of what you have lost. Yes, make a list. Let your mind roll through both insignificant and heavy losses. Which one tugs at you as you prepare to write? Consider writing a haiku about that photograph you lost. Or the frustration of misplacing a credit card. Or use this invitation to explore a more complex loss–in which case you are invited to BEGIN a poem here, and return to it later. Poetry offers a power of processing loss, but it might take more time than we have today. Here is a poem from Allison. It may feel too adult for our students, but we know our teachers and parents of our students have experienced loss from breast cancer, and this poem humanizes teachers, mothers, and women in our lives.

Mentor Poem

"What I Have I Lost" by Allison Berryhill

I did not lose a breast.
I lost my passport.
I lost the diamond from my engagement ring.
I lost the photos of the trip to France
The summer I was 16.
The same summer I lost my friendship with Ann.
But I didn't lose my breast.
The right one
No longer here
Tissue disposed as
Human waste
Burned in the incinerator at the University of Iowa.
It's gone, to be sure.
But I gave it, willing sacrifice.
Not a loss
My soft and tender cup
Of motherhood,
womanhood
Identity.
Its loss (*not loss!*)
Is as precious to me
As the breast itself
Ever was.

7. Aural Textures
Original prompt by Jennifer Guyor Jowett

Inspiration
Jennifer was inspired by the poet Michelle Burke who wrote: "We all have words we love simply because of how they sound." Today, we invite students to play with the sound of words. Rather than focus on the connotation and denotation of words, let's explore aural textures by creating a sound palette. (Learn more about Michelle Burke through the Poetry Foundation.)

Process
- Brainstorm several words, both real and imaginary for each of the following categories (crunchy, billowy, soft, hard, sharp, gravelly, smooth, angular, fluffy).
- Choose words based on their sound rather than their meaning (kick might be crunchy, gall might be billowy).
- Write a poem using these sound words. Challenge yourself to think of the words in relation to their aural texture rather than their denotation.
- Highlight words from the sound palette, including some real and some imaginary
- Have fun with this. Lewis Carroll played with imaginary words to great effect.

Jennifer's Sound Palette:
- Crunchy: chomp, categorize, canny, crack, electric, corkery
- Billowy: blessing, bowlful, imagination, blossoming, promising, bromfully
- Soft: serendipitous, silhouette, shimmering, sandstorm, slippered, salmon, somportent
- Hard: hectoring, heartfelt, atmosphere, duration, huggardly
- Gravelly: gradation, chipper, thunderous, gruffly, gundersone
- Smooth: swarming, shooting, softly, sensual, yellow, hooing
- Angular: righteous, rigorous, empty, twisting, tipidly
- Fluffy: philanthropy, flowering, famously, floundering, fossimossity

Mentor Poem

"The Crack Electric" by Jennifer Guyor Jowett

Ideas blossom into the atmosphere
that is my imagination
like the shooting stars of childhood
sparking into being
one giant flare
a treasure short lived
a surge electric
cracking and thunderous
realized and forming
between fossimossity and reality
bought and sold
a near promise
a wish that almost was
evaporating swiftly
leaving a shimmering trail
hooing its way
across the light-filled expanse
of my mind.

8. Your Weather
Original prompt by Andy Schoenborn

Inspiration

Claudia Rankine wrote her poem <u>"Weather"</u> in response to the tumultuous climate we experienced in the summer of 2020 in America. Inspired by her words, Andy notes that each of us has weather in our lives with which to contend. Weather can be literally the state of the atmosphere, and metaphoric, the larger societal movements that are swirling around. Today, let's write verse about weather.

Process

Is there a storm that you are bearing up against? Write a poem about the weather that surrounds you right now. As you write, identify the moments in your piece you would like readers to pause, consider, and hold onto a bit longer. Use enjambment and italics for impact on these words and lines.

Mentor Poem

"Ravaged" by Barb Edler

Ravaged
Iowa's high humidity
sucks the breath away
pressing down
an all pervasive blanket of sweat that
completely debilitates
Within a few minutes,
temperatures drop thirty degrees
unleashing
a miserable nightmare
of thunderous black clouds
Derecho gnashes its ravenous teeth
roars to life
howls savagely
fiercely devouring all in
its straight line path
Heartlessly
ransacking homes
snapping lines
uprooting trees
whipping loose bolts
into dangerous projectiles
Piercing hearts
Devouring dreams
Silencing satellite towers
Are you okay?
Texts go unanswered;
breathing is an anxious sorrowful sigh
All is flattened
A war zone is left behind
And the rainbows have all died

9. Receiving
Original prompt by Sarah J. Donovan

Inspiration

Receive. A verb. Gerund or past participle: receiving. To be given, presented with, or paid (something). In this case, there is an implication of acceptance or collection. To suffer, experience, or be subjected to (specified treatment). In this case, one is met with, encounters, experiences, undergoes. Think about receiving in the sense of being open to, welcoming in, holding space for (something) that you need, want, wish.

Process

To begin, reflect on and answer a grandiose question - what do you need most in your life right now? Is your answer concrete or abstract? How would having this change things for you? Imagine *receiving* it. By welcoming, accepting the *idea* of this in your life, you might just be manifesting it — or at least *receiving* it during the time you craft your poem today. For the form, think about two stanzas: 1) a stanza of before you received what you manifested, and 2) a stanza after – of your receiving, of its impact on your being.

Mentor Poem

"Nothingness" by Kim Johnson

all sorts
of vise grips
tightening freedom
hindering lingering
clamping rest
choking life
keep me on the move
doing something else
to check another box:
done!

I want some
nothingness

and with it
I'll take
a cup of hot tea
a book
a journal
a pen
a comfy chair
and two wet noses
by a blazing fireplace
savoring each moment
of simple pleasures
cherishing the warmth
of the deep
peace

10. Breath Diamante
Original prompt by Sarah J. Donovan

Inspiration
Breathe. Do nothing for ten minutes, except breathe. Yep. That. That is the inspiration for today. Breath. Breathing. In. Out. And again. And again. We begin with this because we can do this. We do, do this. We breathe. Who knew that it would be a privilege rather than a right, that the pandemic would overcome the airways of our most vulnerable, or that our historically marginalized would be restricted because of systemic injustice. If you can, breathe. Notice and appreciate your breath. In. And. Out. Now, name what you breathe in. What do you want to, need to breathe in, to receive? This may be abstract or concrete. And then name what you breathe out. This may be something toxic in your body or life that you want to expel, or it may be something that you are giving to others, the world. Perhaps what you exhale is a wish or a gift.

Process
Diamante. Or maybe you'd like to try a diamante poem, invented in 1969 by Iris McClellan Tiedt. The antonym diamante poem is a rather accessible formula for students and a great way to illuminate relationships between concrete and abstract concepts and consider white space:
- Line one: Noun
- Line two: Two adjectives that describe the noun in line one
- Line three: Three verbs that end with "ing" and describe the noun's actions or functions in line one
- Line four: Four nouns—the first two must relate to the noun in line one and the second two will relate to the noun in line seven
- Line five: Three verbs that end with "ing" and describe the noun in line seven
- Line six: Two adjectives that describe the noun in line seven
- Line seven: Noun that is opposite in meaning to line one (antonym diamante) or the same in meaning (synonym diamante) as the noun in line one

Mentor Poem

"peace" by Sarah J. Donovan

peace
nourish, heal
sowing, growing, blossoming
breathe in, breathe out
hovering, fluttering, soaring
tend, comfort
gratitude

11. Your Life's a Table of Contents
Original prompt by Kim Johnson

Inspiration

Imagine a table of contents for your poetry collection. Or, imagine a ToC for some other aspect of your life - what you did last year, who's who in your family, what are your favorite pastimes? Let's make a Table of Contents poem today.

Process

Imagine you are creating a book collection of your own life or work. Try your hand at organizing some aspect of your life into chapters and subsections. Feel free to change up this prompt by imagining another book section, say an appendix, glossary, or a list of illustrations. Have fun!

Mentor Poem

"Kindergarten and Jumbo Crayons" by Donnetta D. Norris

Multiple Elementary Schools because we moved a lot.
Loos Elementary and meeting my best friend.
Fairport Intermediate – horrible typing and horrible singing
Patterson Coop: Business Administration which translated into Clerical Skills
Delco Moraine: 2-year Internship where I applied those clerical skills
Bowling Green State University – not the one in Kentucky
Marriage #1 = Child #1
Marriage #2 = Child #2
Army Life as an Army Wife
Webster University – Human Resources Management
Western Governors University – Teaching Certification
Frank Long Elementary
McDonough Elementary
Dutchtown Elementary
Makalapa Elementary
Hobbs Williams Elementary
Roark Elementary
To Be Continued…

12. 100 Words
Original prompt by Andy Schoenborn

Inspiration

Some of the best writing comes from the simplest words. Too often writers rely on multisyllabic words that can have the opposite effect of the writer's desired intent. Today's prompt is to write a 100-word story using only one-syllable words. The poetic twist is to then revise your piece by adding intentional enjambments and spacing that cause the reader's eye to pause and consider the story from a new angle. It's a fun challenge. Are you game?

Process

Write a story of 100 words using only one-syllable words using narrative prose. When finished, read your piece aloud and listen for the moments that make you pause. Honor those moments and revise your piece by adding intentional enjambments and spacing. Example:

> "Still." She said, "Be still, and breathe." Though I did not know her, my lungs drew breath. Mint and a faint waft of salt – strange, yet good. My mind was still. Blood beat in my ears – a drum. A fist, tight and wide, clutched my chest. "Breathe." The word hushed through the dark like a faint hand. "Breathe. Darn it!" A pin prick of light hung like the glow of a lamp. Cold air rushed me and the glow of the light swelled. Light burst and I saw the green eyes of the one who brought me back to life.

Mentor Poem

"Be Still and Breathe" by Andy Schoenborn

"Still," she said,
  "be still, and breathe."

Though I did not know her,
my lungs drew breath.

Mint and a faint waft of salt
- strange, yet good.

My mind was still.
Blood beat in my ears - a drum.
A fist, tight and wide,
clutched my chest.

"Breathe."

The word hushed through the dark
like a faint hand.

"Breathe. Darn it!"

A pin prick of light
hung like the glow of a lamp.

Cold air rushed me
and the glow of the light swelled.

Light burst and I saw the green eyes
of the one who brought
me back to life.

13. Written on a Shirt
Original prompt by Britt Decker

Inspiration

Britt's mom would bring home little trinkets and, almost always, a T-shirt whenever mom traveled anywhere without her. The T-shirt often had the name of the city she'd visited or something related to books. As Britt writes, our T-shirts tell stories. A simple shirt, or the statement we can make based on the words we choose to wear, creates a connection with others.

Process

1. Are you wearing inspiration today? Or, do you have a favorite T-shirt that offers a special statement? Use this quote, saying, phrase, or picture to instigate your poem.
2. Write a poem in any form inspired by your selected shirt.
3. If acquired when traveling, consider incorporating the memory
4. If acquired as a gift, consider incorporating your relationship to that person

Mentor Poem

"Distance" by Britt Decker

I kept colleagues at a
d i s t a n c e
Work and home need
boundaries
These three wormed their
way into my classroom,
into my phone,
into my happy hour,
into my home
When the days are long,
when the load feels too much,
the squad lifts me up
with notes, with coffee, with belly laughs,
with presence and understanding

14. What I Didn't Do
Original prompt by Tammy Breitweiser

Inspiration

It is good to let go of, give up, and/or say goodbye to things we have outgrown. Things that no longer make sense. Things that are not good for us. What's on your list? Naomi Shihab Nye's "Burning the Old Year" is a wonderful mentor poem that you should feel free to check out. Think about what has come and gone. What do you release and what do you hold onto in your life?

Process

Write a list of the things you haven't accomplished. Consider what ideas you need to burn and let go. If you have access to Naomi Shihab Nye's poem, write down what images strike you from the poem. What images from your life and memory does her poem bring forth? Make a list of these images.

Freewrite for 10 minutes considering the notes you made. Reread and mark at least 4 phrases that sparkle for you. Use those phrases in your poem in a different order.

Mentor Poem

"Burn it Down" by Tammy Breitweiser

Coffee, black stains the blood red shirt
The doorway stands and holds me up,
sturdy , the color of chocolate,
Silent and safe.
So much not done these days,
Lists of tasks moved on the calendar
From one day to the next week,
Gray swirls of smoke
That take the logic and thoughts
Away.
Now that you are gone
There is no trip to New York,
Or pro baseball games,
Or a plane ride anywhere.
Grief swallows and spits
The ashes of the life
That is now burnt to
Ash.

15. Let's Take a Walk
Original prompt by Leilya Pitre

Inspiration

Perhaps you are tired, if not exhausted, of daily work, responsibilities, and multiple commitments. It is challenging to juggle our lives at times. We all need a break. For our poetry today, let's take a walk, a mental walk. Yes, really. A walk is a time for reflection and relaxation. It is time to accept, forget, and forgive. It is time to recharge and restore your balance. You may take us to any place, a dear moment in your life, or walk us through your favorite food preparation.

Process

Close your eyes and imagine walking to your favorite place of comfort. Write a walk poem that is instigated by one of the following:

1. You may write about different things that attract your attention during the walk;
2. You may write about the walk that resulted in some important personal revelation;
3. You may write about the walk into the past—a place or time—that brings you comfort, delight, or help face struggles;
4. You may write a poem that mirrors the length, style, and shape of the actual walk.

There is no specific pattern, count of syllables, or rhyme requirements. Freestyle!

Mentor Poem

"Navigational Mnemonic" by Glenda Funk

some folk never amble past the fence post marking their
postage stamp corner of the planet.
some folk never wend their way where forest pheromones
release stress reducing aerosols, where Quaking aspen shimmy
flat leaves and whisper in light breezes.
some folks never stroll through word-canopies or take their
anxious amygdala past electronic outposts on uncharted paths
leading to aha horizons.
some folks slog only through their known worlds, their minds
shelved, dusty & undiscovered; their feet anchored & moored.
unlike some folks i pootle & promenade, traipse & toddle,
stride & stretch my legs. dreaming of new ways to walk along
my daily path I hunker into poetry's navigational mnemonics.

References

Berryhill, A. (2020, February 17). February 4/5 : what have you lost? Ethical ELA. https://www.ethicalela.com/february-day-4-5-what-have-you-lost/

Breitweiser, T. (2022, April 20). What I didn't do. Ethical ELA. https://www.ethicalela.com/what-i-didnt-do/

Decker, B. (2023, February 21). Written on a shirt. Ethical ELA. https://www.ethicalela.com/written-on-a-shirt/

Donovan, S. (2020, November 16). Receiving. Ethical ELA. https://www.ethicalela.com/receiving/

Donovan, S. (2020, November 17). Breath. Ethical ELA. https://www.ethicalela.com/breath/

Harrison, A. (2023, April 28). Come, join my reality. Ethical ELA. https://www.ethicalela.com/come-join-my-reality/

Ingalls, S. (2022, April 27). Re-encounters. Ethical ELA. https://www.ethicalela.com/re-encounters/

Johnson, K. (2020, May 20). Right words at the right time. Ethical ELA. https://www.ethicalela.com/may-openwrite-right-words-at-the-right-time/

Johnson, K. (2021, March 15). Your life's a table of contents. Ethical ELA. https://www.ethicalela.com/your-lifes-table-of-contents/

Jowett, J. (2020, March 14). March, day 1/5 : aural textures. Ethical ELA. https://www.ethicalela.com/march-auraltextures/

Jowett, J. (2023, April 4). Grammatically ungrammatical. Ethical ELA. https://www.ethicalela.com/grammatically-ungrammatical/

Joy, S. L. (2023, April 3). What a wonderful world of words. ELA. https://www.ethicalela.com/15437-2/

Pitre, L. (2022, April 21). When you need a break, go to a place of comfort. Ethical ELA. https://www.ethicalela.com/when-you-need-a-break-go-to-a-place-of-comfort/

Schoenborn, A. (2019, October 17). October: 5/5 day writing challenge. Ethical ELA. https://www.ethicalela.com/october-5-5-day-writing-challenge/

Schoenborn, A. (2020, August 17). August #openwrite: your weather. Ethical ELA. https://www.ethicalela.com/august-openwrite-your-weather/

Resources

Consider exploring these resources on your own or with your school or local librarian if you want to further reference them or have them handy for your students.

Mountain, A. *"Drift."* https://poets.org/poem/drift

Bitsui, S. https://www.poetryfoundation.org/poets/sherwin-bitsui

Bitsui, S. (2020, November 24). Arts and culture: poems by Sherman Bitsui. NAU: Northern Arizona University. https://nau.edu/stories/sherwin-bitsui-poetry/

Rankine, C. (2020, June 15). Poem:'*Weather'* *https://www.nytimes.com/2020/06/15/books/review/claudia-rankine-weather-poem-coronavirus.html*

Nye, N.S. *"Burning the Old Year.".* https://www.poetryfoundation.org/poems/48597/burning-the-old-year

Chapter 6: Walking the World

Dear Teacher,

We imagine this letter finds you well into the school year. You know your students poetically; they know you, and they know one another in ways only poets do. We hope the "Healing Ways" section serves to nurture all your hearts and minds and that the poetry that fills the pages of the paper or digital notebooks you've cultivated brings joy and wonder --- perhaps a readiness for some exploration beyond the classroom and into the world.

A turn toward the world is not an endeavor to begin without careful thought about your community and the worldly connections that extend from the world into your classroom. In Sarah's community, there is a large population of students displaced by war. In some of our teacher-friends' schools in border towns, we know that students' lives are not limited to a state or country. Many of our students' worlds are wildly expansive beyond what we experienced as youth because of the digital spaces our students travel every day, sharing their passions across the globe and meeting influencers eager to engage with our students.

Writing poetry about the world – digital and physical spaces -- encourages students to observe art, culture, events, weather, animals, technology (you name it) from the perspective of a global citizen. So this section draws on all the perspective-taking poetry they wrote in "Becoming Us" and "Welcoming Neighbors." The heightened awareness that poetic thinking can bring leads to a greater appreciation of our environment and an increased sense of compassion, maybe even empathy.

Writing poetry about the world or places that may seem "other" to our students supports care in the words we use to describe people, places, and experiences beyond our lived lives. Encouraging students to do inquiry into people and places in other countries also gives students a literary space to voice their concerns, hopes, and dreams for our shared world. In a poem, students can address important societal issues, express their opinions, and inspire change. Poetry can also serve as a call to action and a means of raising awareness about global and local challenges.

By making space in the school year for students to write about the world, we are prompting them to think critically about the issues that matter to them in other places and for other people. This process of introspection to extrospection and the unfolding of life in other parts of the world. Finally, the poetry students write during this phase of their poetic journey contributes to the literary world as they make poems that will help their classmates see the world in new poetic ways because of shared and varied interests.

There are several prompts here that ask you and your students to do an inquiry into the news or the World Wide Web. Of course, we offer suggested resources for student exploration that have worked for us in our contexts. Still, we recommend that you take care with these prompts and offer trusted websites or a library database that minimizes graphic images or harmful content.

Peace,

Sarah, Mo, & Maureen

1. Origin Stories
Original prompt by Jennifer Guyor Jowett

Inspiration

Several writers have given us a glimpse of their origins, their words evoking the sounds, smells, and touch of the world as they came into being. Use one of these writers as inspiration (Brian Komei Dempster's *Origin*, Jacqueline Woodson's opening lines of *Brown Girl Dreaming*, George Ella Lyon's *I'm From*) and delve deeply into your own origins.

Process

- Read through the Origin Story poem examples.
- Select a format that resonates with you or use the mentor poem.
- Use a literary device, such as anaphora, to ground readers into the origin.
- Explore the richness of the world you birthed from, considering the contrast between the place you originated and what runs through you.

Mentor Poem

"Familia" by Sarah J. Donovan

Through silencing they came,
shrouded in second-class skin,
scarred by myopic glances
and iron fists, they
crushed their bosom with books,
pinched pain into pastries,
splashed fury in Moscato pours
for Papa, Mio figlio. I
place a lilac branch in my legacy,
a terra cotta vase
from my grandmother's village,
hand-painted with Tuscan spring wildflowers–
Dolores and Adele, daughters
for whom she kept secrets, told half-truths,
stole from church coffers for school Papa refused
while Mio figlio
devoured contrition-filled ravioli.
I resisted the kitchen, turned from men,
pushed books into my bosom, dwelled alone.
What is the value of a girl?
Silence. Dolores and Adele
inherited Papa's myopic gaze
uttering Mio figlio
not in pride but disdain, favoring their girls,
depriving their boys of affection,
draining husbands of their virility.
I pinch a cluster of four petal blossoms–
Grandma, Dolores, Adele, Sarah.
Fragrant lilac drifts from the vase,
vines connecting, strangling
the painted wildflowers.
What is the value of a girl?

2. A Poet Like Me
Original prompt by Anna J. Small Roseboro

Inspiration

One reason we celebrate VerseLove in April is that William Shakespeare, the Bard, was born in this month. This is not the only birth month for clever poets. Look at you. Other well-known poets were born in the same month as you. You know that students are intrigued when invited to write Golden Shovel poems because they get to choose the poet, the line or phrase, the style, and often the topic about which to write. Our prompt today offers our writers the same choices.

Process

So, today let's mine for a line to craft a Golden Shovel poem extracted and quoted from a poem written by a poet who was born the same month as you.   If April is your month, go ahead and mine a line from the Bard. Choose a poet like you because you were born in the same month. For easy access, consider one of these sites:
- https://www.bornglorious.com/united_states/birthday/?pd=today
- https://junebirthdaysofpoets.wordpress.com/ (substitute your birth month in the URL>

Choose a poem by that poet. Select a line or phrase you find innovative, evocative, or just clever. Use that line or phrase in your poem on a topic of your choice in at least one of these ways.
- as a refrain at least three times in your poem
- as the first line in a pantoum poem.
- as the first or last word in lines of your poem so that reading from first to last line, we see those quoted words in the order they appeared in the model poem of the poet like you.
- as inspiration for your poem.

Please cite as an opening or closing comment, the poet and poem as well as the chosen line or phrase. AND…if time permits, insert a picture or graphic that expands our understanding of your poet, your chosen lines, phrase, or the theme or message of your poem.

Mentor Poem

Denise Krebs chose a striking line for her golden shovel from Rita Dove's "Ars Poetica": "What I want is this poem to be small."

Ars Poetica

What a poem needs
I wouldn't presume to know, but I
want it to brandish truth.
Is that okay to ask?
This fearful world needs a
poem to smack us alive,
to resuscitate trust, to
be a balm for large (even
small) wounds of our soul.

3. Giving Voice
Original prompt by Jennifer Guyor Jowett

Inspiration

Today, we're raising up voice while considering how people are recognized. To really explore this pairing, we must push toward brutal honesty, explore that which might be dismissed. We must become the voice.

Process

Using Naomi Shihab Nye's poem "A Palestinian Might Say" as a launching point, play around with the idea of what you recognize individually. Build from this singular recognition by adding details that provoke others to see it too. Push into the setting, its life, letting the voice build upon itself in a cumulative catalog, allowing the reader to see from the inside: What?/You don't feel at home in your country,/almost overnight?/All the simple things/you cared about,/maybe took for granted. . ./you feel/insulted, invisible?/Almost as if you're not there?

Mentor Poem

"An Automobile Might Say" by Ruth Reneau

Despite my constant warnings
You choose not to listen
To my echoing cries
Instead you willfully hasten
To your daily routine
And the nerve to return at evening
With you usual fancy and demanding
Not caring of my plight
Even if it affects your flight
Until I refuse to move further
Then some sense you gather
In the midst of heavy traffic
You act as if I work magic
Oh no! I cant help you now
It is out of my hands somehow

4. The Room Where It Happens
Original prompt comes from Alexis Ennis

Inspiration

The Broadway show, *Hamilton,* came to Alexis' area and she was able to attend a show. Every time she hears this music, her love of history is immediately reignited. She initially wanted to be a history teacher in the hopes that she could teach what happened in history and bring history to life in an engaging way. She has always loved history-from her early love of *American Girl* books and *Out of the Dust,* to a job shadowing at a local museum. When Alexis went to college, her eyes were opened to the history that she was not taught, or that was brushed over so quickly that its importance was lost to her. Alexis' eyes were opened and her heart yearned to bring that awareness and love to youth. Although she currently teaches computers and technology, her love of showing students the truth and her hope to inspire a love of learning is still strong.

All that is to say, let's bring history alive through poetry! If you need inspiration or have yet to listen to Hamilton, put this soundtrack on repeat and get inspired. We promise you will.

Process

Bring us to the "Room Where it Happens" and research a historical figure that you can bring to life in a poem. The poem can be short or long, rhyming or non. Have fun with it and bonus points if you can bring to life a figure that has been hidden from the pages for too long.

Mentor Poem

"Attempt for Amna Al Haddad" by Stefani Boutelier

Amna lifted barriers
women who weight-ed generations
to heave oppression
misogyny, citing religion
unapproved athletic clothing
Amna didn't bomb out
she hooked it, snatched it
attention at the worlds

5. Found Poems in International News
Original prompt by Amy Vetter

Inspiration

We can find inspiration in the everyday words that we read. Maybe those words and phrases are from novels that we are reading that help us make sense of ourselves and the world around us. Or maybe those words and phrases are from speeches or articles that we rearrange to speak back to a narrative that is not serving us. Found poems offer us the space to do both.

Process

A found poem is like a collage. The writer finds words, phrases, and lines from everyday texts, such as newspaper articles, letters, social media, graffiti, etc. A found poet takes those words and refashions or rearranges them into another poem. The poem can take any form, so feel to rhyme or not. To start, find a text (e.g. a novel) or series of texts (e.g., novel, poem, article) and pull out words, phrases, sentences that stick out to you. Play around with the words. Rearrange them until a thought or theme jumps out at you. Continue until you've created a cohesive text.

Mentor Poem

"Russia's Invasion of The Ukraine According to My Facebook Feed"
by Amy Vetter

Putin's tracks,
heightened alert.
This is NOT Russia!
Still not Russa!
Does it look like Russia?

Dear people of Ukraine,
the President is not an icon,
or an idol or a portrait.
I am here.
We are not putting down arms.
Our weapon is truth.
Ceasefire and withdraw.

Dear people of Ukraine,
the world will hold Russia accountable.
Switzerland sets aside its long tradition of neutrality.
U.S. imposes sanctions like no other.
Britain sends antitank weapons.
Elon Musk pledges to send Starlink terminals.

Dear people of Ukraine,
Your unbreakable spirit
352 civilians, including 14 children, dead,
metro stations turned bomb shelters,
a baby was born in the underground.
Praying for peace.
My heart aches.
Pity.

And when they bombed other people's houses,
we lived happily during the war.
I took a chair outside and watched the sun.

NOTE: The last stanza is taken from We Lived Happily During the
War BY ILYA KAMINSKY.

6. Today Years Old
Original poem from Scott McCloskey

Inspiration

Have you heard of the saying, "I was today years old when I found out about….."? It's what we say when we find out something surprising, something new that we've just learned. For instance, did you know that snails have the most teeth of any animal in the world? The Rainbow Slug (essentially a snail without a shell) can have as many as 700,000 teeth. That's a lot of teeth. Or did you know that ceiling fans have a switch on the side so you can change their directions, which you should do depending on the season (clockwise in winter and counterclockwise in summer)? Isn't being a life-long learner pretty cool? There's new stuff to learn every day! Let's use this to our advantage!

Process

Find something interesting about a place or being existing in another part of the world or start here with a list of thirty stunning facts: Bored Panda. Use it in a free verse poem. You could examine the facts. Interrogate it. Expand on it. Or simply just share it with the rest of us. Have your students research a topic, find an interesting "fact" and then explore that "fact" in a poem. You could even have them cite their sources so you (and your other students) could learn more about the given (or self-chosen) topics.]

Mentor Poem
"Toxoplasmosis" by Scott McCloskey

Watching an episode
of Chicago Med,
I realize that some
cat owners have a
single-celled parasite
in their brains that
compel them to
take care of their cats.

I smile, looking over
at you, curled
on the couch,
wife of mine
for over twenty-five
years, arm crooked
around the Kindle,
half watching,
half reading,
and I think, this
is gold, I can use
this, fashion
it into a poem
about attraction,
about want and need,
about how deeply
I love you,

but I just can't seem
to get past the notion
of consent – or lack
thereof – if I'm being
"made" to love you or
if it's my own free will,
and besides
there's the problem
that this parasite
is excreted
by the cats
in their feces,
and no amount
of linguistic wordplay
could get passed that.

7. Island Earth
Original poem by Emily Cohn

Inspiration

In his book, *The Natty Professor,* Tim Gunn tells us inspiration can come from anywhere. Emily's shower curtain becomes a map of islands that surround her own, with fantastic names like Fling Island, and Brimstone Island, and she starts to daydream about these places. Take a trip to a real or imagined island today!

Process

- Remember an island: real, fictional, ancestral, or otherwise.
- Find an island.
- Invent an island you want to go to or want to avoid.
- Or read Islands by Yusef Komunyakaa and take a line or word with you.
- Imagine or describe a world there.

Free verse might suit you. Or perhaps a form will inspire new thoughts? Try a cinquain if you'd like:
- Line 1: 2 syllables
- Line 2: 4 syllables
- Line 3: 6 syllables
- Line 4: 8 syllables
- Line 1: 2 syllables

Feel free to add or subtract a syllable from each line. It's your island, make the rules!

Mentor Poem

"Butter Island" by Emily Cohn

Butter Island
Corn cliffs
Yellow cream shore
Cooling your toasted feet
Dip your lobster in the tidepools
Sweet land

8. Nonet Technology News
Original prompt by Sarah J. Donovan

Inspiration

A nonet is a nine-line poem. A nonet can be written on any subject and rhyming is optional. The poem starts with a line that has 9 syllables in it. The second line contains 8 syllables, the third line has 7 syllables, and it continues to count down to one syllable in the final line (ninth line).

Process

Search images and news outlets for the latest innovations in technology. Is there an issue in the world that interests you (e.g., education, family time, access to water, protecting coral reefs, war, poverty, racism, police brutality, politics, immigration, global warming, guns, freedom, refugees, gender) consider the role of technology in solving or complicating that issue? Tell a story or describe what's happening in a nonet.

Mentor Poem

This is the article followed by my nonet:
https://newsela.com/articles/syria-chemical-weapon-attack/id/28950/

"Sarin Gas" by Sarah J. Donovan

Sarin gas breathed in or touched cripples
human's central nervous system.
The dark side of science when
chemicals kill not heal
weaponized by men
to suffocate
our children
for what?
Land?

9. Ecopoetry PostScripts
Original prompt by Jennifer Guyor Jowett

Inspiration
One of the prevalent concerns many students have is climate change, which creates an eco-anxiety amongst them. Jennifer began exploring ways students could confront their concerns through writing and landed in the world of ecopoetry, poems about ecology, environmental injustice, and climate change.

This exploration led to an essay written by Craig Santos Perez, a teacher and indigenous Chamoru from the Pacific Island of Guam. He works to "highlight how poetry can communicate environmental issues through creative language and expressive form… and can put a human face and emotional experience on abstract natural disaster and climate crises." Jennifer especially loved that the work he does "becomes a form of literary eco-activism." One of his students stated, "Ecopoetry inspires us to act" and that inspires hope. (I'm sure Emily Dickinson would approve).

Process
- You might begin by listing what concerns you most about the environment.
- You might consider adding a collective noun as a way of connecting to the natural world.
- You might start as Perez suggests: reading and watching science journalism that focuses on the environment and annotating key words, facts, and descriptions to create a basis for your poem.
- You might take inspiration from a diversity of poets to reflect the biodiversity of our world.
- You might reflect upon the impact humans have on the environment, bringing an awareness that causes a desire to take action.
- You might consider writing your poem as a form of postscript.
- The form is up to you. As always, we invite you to write from your heart in whatever way offers hope or inspires you to act today.

Mentor Poem

"A Murder of Crows" by Jennifer Guyor Jowett

the sky is full of crows
black shadows
slashing the air
leaving gashes behind

until

they land
picking pieces of straw
from the scarecrows
we've become

while

we hang limp
in the fields
watching over
the world we planted

10. Weathering the News
Original prompt from Susie Morice

Inspiration

Today's news is pliant, often leaving us wanting the fuller story, the truth. The news gets our adrenaline pumped. Today, use the news. Susie used Martin Espada's poem, his close examination of the news of Mario Gonzalez Arenales, and also a new feature in the Sunday NYT on Long Covid. Espada takes a grim circumstance, narrating a much deeper reality through his poem. And Sharon Otterman gives us "Fighting Long Covid to Work Again" (NYT, Feb. 27, 2022). During the height of the pandemic, Susie wondered about the long-term psychological impact of life in Covidlandia. These two inspirations might trigger your own response to a news piece. News is powerful and a marvelous catalyst for poetic response.

Process

Look up the weather (or alternatively another section of the news like sports) in a national or international newspaper. See how the news reports your state or maybe you have family from Mexico or India. Search up the weather report in those parts of the world. Use the news piece as a launch for a poem that conveys the article's concerns that this news arouses. Tell the news report in a poem or try to use simile to describe what was happening. See how Erica writes about tornadoes in her home state of Arkansas.

Mentor Poem

"Four suspected tornadoes hit Arkansas" by Erica Johnson

As if they were a posse of bandits
straight out of the wild west.
riding in under cover of darkness,
but causing quite the scene,
you listen for the oncoming train
hearing only a plea for shelter.

"We watched as the tornado pass."
As if they were classmates in the hall,
the school bullies that hurl insults
like golf-ball sized hail
and may not leave injuries,
but you tremble alone
in your bathroom all the same.

11. Recuerdos de Comida y Amor
Original prompt by Stacey L. Joy

Inspiration

Who is your favorite Latinx poet, author, educator, activist, artist, or human? Or perhaps there is a Latinx poet you want to know more about. Explore here for a start. When we read Pablo Neruda's "Ode to My Socks," we think of all the memories food and clothing hold for us. In the spirit of all the Latinx influences in our lives and possibly our communities (Stacey's for sure), imagine how dull and empty life would be without those contributions/inspirations. Stacey grew up on a street named Don Felipe, not far from the street where she teaches now named Obama Blvd. formerly Rodeo Road. Every day, she drives on La Cienega and La Brea. She eats tacos, burritos, guacamole, and salsa more than any American food. Reflect on your community, food, artwork, your school curriculum, your childhood, etc., and find some Latinx inspiration to help you write today.

Process

Make a list of things that you found in your memories that have Latinx roots or inspirations. Perhaps you might want to write an ode to an object like Neruda's or to someone's actions like Elizabeth Acevedo's "Ode to the Head Nod". Maybe you will find a strike line from a Latinx poem and compose a Golden Shovel. How about a love letter (an epistola, Latin word for letter) to an object, person, or event?

Mentor Poem

"Mis Héroes" by Mo Daley

If it weren't for
the chivalry of Miguel Cervantes de Saavedra,
the otherworldly women of Isabel Allende,
the lyricism and versatility of Sandra Cisneros,
the introspective journeys of Ana Castillo,
the magical mysticism of Gabriel Garcia Márquez,
the explored history of Maria Vargas Llosa,
the heartbreaking Mariposas of Julia Alvarez,
the healing souls of Rudolfo Anaya,
the preternatural recipes of Laura Esquivel,
the experimental prose of Julio Cortázar,
the grim borderlands of Luis Alberto Urrea,
the fearless, honest voice of Elizabeth Acevedo,
who would I be?

12. Embodying Global Art
Original prompt by Scott McCloskey

Inspiration
We were reminded of a Billy Collins' poem "Introduction to Poetry" which is a rather haunting poem about a woman who was "in" the poem, a photograph or painting, but also wasn't. (This, of course, was Margaret Atwood's powerful and somber "This Is a Photograph of Me.") Scott got to thinking about photography and paintings and "embodying" those works of art. So, here we are today.

Process
We'd like you to find a painting you're "drawn to" for whatever reason and then, à la Billy Collins's "Introduction to Poetry," step into it. If you remember his instructions to his students from stanza four – "[W]alk inside the poem's room / and feel the walls for a light switch" – that's what we will try today. Find a painting, enter the painting – choose a perspective from something/someone in the piece – and write about it.

You can find some artwork here: Google Arts & Culture. There's a lot to see on this site. Try not to be overwhelmed. If you click on Explore (at the top), you'll be able to find Art Camera (or just click on those words), and that will get you closer to actually examining some works of art. The poems we've mentioned could all serve as wonderful Mentor Poems, but if you'd like one more, here's one by Allen Ginsberg about a Cézanne painting: "Cézanne's Ports."

When "stepping into the painting," you could take the perspective of someone in the painting. You could take the perspective of someone not in the painting, too, someone just "off camera," as it were. Or what about the artist herself? What about the patron who commissioned the work? You could even delve a bit into the background of the work itself and explore/interrogate that in your poem. Choose whatever poetic "format" you'd like.

Mentor Poem

The strike line for this Golden Shovel came from the
description of Frida Kahlo's green bow: The dull green
tone reflects for her the color of the leaves and sadness:
Frida is in mourning.

"the unibrow bird mourns" by Stacey L. Joy

longing for a life filled with the
freedom to fly away from this dull
loveless sky. Soaring above green
troubled lands buried in revolution. Soothing is the tone
of her spider monkey, who reflects
both of their yearnings for
love. He mirrors the suffering in her
as her alter ego. the
dark muted brushstrokes and color
on the canvas of
her existence reveal how the
anguish never leaves
but soaks and
stains their lives of
sadness:

Frida, your being
is a reflection of life and strength while
in a state of pain, distress and
mourning

13. These Poems
Original prompt by Sarah Donovan

Inspiration
W.H. Auden once wrote: "Poets who want to change the world tend to be unreadable." In a conversation between Pearl London and June Jordan, Jordan had something to say about that quote. She called that "elitist" and said that "you have to be accessible to people on the first reading or first hearing on some level…and when they reread it something else can happen again."

There was a fundamental shift in poetry in the US around the 60s with writing in the black arts communities. And then anti-Vietnam War movement — all kinds of poets who never wrote anything political were writing war poems to be read at rallies by thousands of people. And, yes, the women's movement. Poetry had to be accessible to engage an audience. Read June Jordan's poem "These Poems" (on poets.org).

Process
Jordan's poem is free verse with a few words on each line. So short. There are three stanzas that begin with "These" — poems, words, skeletal lines. Each word is a synonym of sorts and yet holds different meanings. Then the final two stanzas show the purpose, the relationality between the poet and the reader with some intimacy and anonymity. Wow.

Some of us write to move an audience. Others are writing to move ourselves. For Sarah, it is somewhere in between. Knowing Sarah has an audience is what makes her write. That her words will land somewhere. That her poem will have a witness in the world.

What are "these" poems you write? Where do you write them? What metaphor works for what your poems are (for Jordan, "they are stones in the water/running away: and "desperate arms)?

Another approach is to think of what "these" poems you have been writing all year do for your understanding of your place in the world. What do "these" poems do for your heart and mind? Maybe you have a favorite poet and want to gather the accessible lines that you carry with you.

Mentor Poem

"F & J" by Sarah J. Donovan

These poems
they are things that I do
in the corner
stroking f & j
begging a seed
becomes something
to remind me
to live.

These fingers–
swelling at night,
aching in knuckles–
feel no pain
tapping letters
into a poem.

These ticks
they are hollow beats
of my heart wishing
to be heard.

I am alive
practicing living
with every letter.

14. Succinct Truth
Original prompt by Maureen Ingram Young

Inspiration
We offer the mentor poet Lucille Clifton and her voluminous poetry. Lucille Clifton began writing poetry at the age of 10 and published some 13 volumes and numerous children's books. The body of her work is hopeful and caring, despite wrestling with difficult issues of family, race, womanhood, abuse, death, and more. She had a unique ability to write concisely; most of her poems measure twenty lines or less, with individual lines only a few words long. It is said that Lucille Clifton, a mother of six, wrote her poetry right in the midst of her busy family life – and she was known to quip, "Why do you think my poems are so short?" We recommend you share this video, if there is time, where Lucille Clifton offers her explanation of what poetry is. Essentially, poetry helps us make sense of, or at least acknowledge the difficulty of sense in, understanding the world.

Process
What issues are going on in the world today that are stirring your heart or mind?

Be inspired by Lucille Clifton and dare to make time to write about it, with both wonder and truth, in the midst of all that needs doing.
- Write down your subject – what angers, challenges, disappoints, hurts, or bugs you?
- Write your poem from your point of view, using a lowercase "i" for yourself.
- Offer a clear, simple, direct image of the problem (when do you experience this? What is happening?)
- How might you weave in a message of hope?
- Limit yourself to 10-20 lines, with short lines (suggestion – reread your draft with a critical eye as to what words are superfluous, unnecessary?)
- Consider playing around with or simply eliminating punctuation and capitalization
- Try to enjoy the puzzling-out of a tough topic with fragments and questions! You don't need to have answers.

Mentor Poem

"If Microphones" by Maureen Ingram Young

i think it would be awesome
if microphones had
lie detectors
then when
politicians pontificate
their voices project
as Minions singing
as cassette tapes rewound
as simply falsetto singing
we'd be united in
enlightenment
we need an app for this

15. X Marks the Spot
Original prompt by Mo Daley

Inspiration
In the summer of 2023, Mo was lucky to attend the Poetry Foundation's Summer Poetry Teachers Institute. We recommend you look into this opportunity for your own professional learning some summer. In a small group session, teachers were given this prompt--X Marks the Spot-- which Mo thought could be a great way to incorporate poetry across the curriculum at every grade level. You could even consider it a formative or summative assessment if you'd like. At this point in the school year, you likely have colleagues asking you about integrating poetry, so you might share this prompt with your History or Science teacher-neighbor.

Process
Find a print article from a magazine that interests you or concerns a classroom topic. Share the article on your learning management platform (Google Classroom, Canvas) or prepare enough copies of different articles so that each student has their own. Once you have chosen your article, simply draw an X through the page. You will then write your poem using the words touching your X. It may be helpful to list selected words and cross them off as they are used. What a great way for students to show what they have learned about the world! Mo italicized the words from the article in her mentor poem.

Mentor Poem

"The Bucket Is Almost Empty" by Mo Daley

I opened *the* various news *accounts last* night
and read about *water, gallons* and gallons of *water*
flowing
through *cities*
and towns
down *mountains*
through canyons
Rios Grandes
and not so grande
confronting us
creating *divides.*
This *is* a *watershed* moment
for our *country.*
How have we *managed* to get to this *point?*
Can our government *squash* the floods?
Will they form yet another *commission*
to keep the *Rio* out,
to keep it *"downstream?"*
Who *knows* what *account* Fox News will give
of this *withdrawal.*
We have so much, *while in* other countries,
county after county,
more than *half* of the people
are *hit* with drought.
When will we see that we are *users?*
Water cannot be *owned.*
We must *exact* from this planet only what we need,
giving more than we take.

References

Cohn, E. (2023, April 22). Island earth. Ethical ELA.
https://www.ethicalela.com/island-earth/

Daley, M. (2024, July 22). X marks the spot. Ethical ELA.
https://www.ethicalela.com/?p=17030

Donovan, S. (2025, June 15). These poems. Ethical ELA.
https://www.ethicalela.com/these-poems/

Donovan, S.J. (2019. Nov. 14). Nonet. Ethical ELA.
https://www.ethicalela.com/november-5-day-
monthly-writing-challenge/

Young, M.I. (2022, April 18). Succinct truth. Ethical ELA.
https://www.ethicalela.com/succinct-truth-inspired-
by-lucille-clifton/

Jowett, J. (2020, March 17). Origin stories. Ethical ELA.
https://www.ethicalela.com/march-day-4-5-origin-
stories/

Jowett, J. (2023, June 18). Ecopoetry postscripts. Ethical
ELA.https://www.ethicalela.com/ecopoetry-
postscripts/

Jowett. J. (2020, March 16). Giving voice. Ethical ELA.
https://www.ethicalela.com/march-day-3-5-giving-
voice/

Ennis, A. (2023, April 23). The room where it happened.
Ethical ELA. https://www.ethicalela.com/15412-2/

Joy, S.L. (223, Sept. 16). Recuerdos de comida y amor. Ethical
ELA. https://www.ethicalela.com/recuerdos-de-
comida-y-amor-memories-of-food-and-love/

McCloskey, S. (2022, August 24). Today years old. Ethical
ELA.https://www.ethicalela.com/today-years-old/

McCloskey, S. (2023, August 22). Embodying art. Ethical ELA. https://www.ethicalela.com/embodying-art/

Morice, S. (2022, April 12). The news. Ethical ELA. https://www.ethicalela.com/the-news/

Roseboro, A. (2023, April 12). A poet like me. Ethical ELA. https://www.ethicalela.com/a-poet-like-me/

Vetter, A. (2022, April 26). Found poems. Ethical ELA. https://www.ethicalela.com/found-poems/

Chapter 7: Reflecting on Moving Poetically

Dear Teacher,

As the school year comes to an end, it's time to reflect on the ways we have used poetry this year. In this section, you will find an assortment of poem prompts that continue to challenge you and your students as you grow as poets this year. You will find a variety of poetic forms and topics. Take some time to think about, write, and discuss your growth. Are you willing to tackle topics and forms that might have caused you some trepidation earlier in the year? We hope that as you have opened your minds and hearts, you have nurtured a safe and welcoming community for your writers.

This section will give you a chance to flex your poetic muscles as you consider your own writing practices. We also wanted to offer some prompts that will encourage students to reread some of their classmates' poems and pay tribute to them in prompts such as "Borrowed Lines" and "Ode to a Poet." To bolster confidence while trying new forms, we have chosen some forms that may be new to your students, such as the tanka, bop, monotetra, and pantoum. After all, your students have been writing all year. This is the perfect time to show them that their poetic lives should extend well beyond the classroom.

In this section, we invite you to have students consider how they have moved poetically through the school year.

How might they continue to move poetically throughout their lives? How will their poetic view shape their writing? While discussing this book, Co-Editor Maureen Young Ingram said, "We have radical goals, turning our students into observers and changemakers of our world." Please take some time to ponder if writing poetry is accomplishing this goal.

Peace,

Sarah, Mo, & Maureen

1. A Space to Look and Think
Original prompt by Katrina Morrison

Inspiration

Katrina finds inspiration in the story "A House of My Own" from Sandra Cisneros's *A House on Mango Street*. The speaker in the story describes her perfect house in detail. She vividly imagines the things she wants to surround herself with so she can have a place to "look and think."

Process

Have students create a mental snapshot of their place to "look and think." Create a list of those things and build a poem around the list. Alternatively, students could create a list of items that make them look back and think, as Katrina did in her mentor poem.

Mentor Poem

"Cabinet" by Katrina Morrison

The contents of
The cabinet
A Gumby but not a Pokey
A red, plastic Captain Kangaroo cup with
those eyes that seem to change
Direction when you move
the cup back and forth
Cat-eye marbles
Jacks and a red rubber ball
A miniature wooden gavel from
a high school
Service organization
A neglected cribbage board
Baoding balls from
A once-in-a-lifetime trip to
San Francisco
A tiny windmill in Delft blue
Memories

2. Free Writing

Original prompt by Margaret Simon

Inspiration

Margaret was inspired by a quote from Martha Graham, who discussed the creative life force within us that could be lost forever if we choose not to share it with the world. The quote can be found at *The Marginalian.*

Process

Margaret asks us to consider roadblocks to our creativity. What can keep us from being creative? How can we let those annoyances go? Margaret suggests free writing. No form, no instructions, just pick up the pen and flow for at least 10 minutes. When you are done, share what you have written. Margaret's poem is one she spoke into her Notes app while on a walk.

Mentor Poem

"Notes from a Walk" by Margaret Simon

I want to pick up a pile of oak leaves
the pile of leaves blown from the curb,
rejected into the street.
I want to hold
a gathering of leaves in my hands,
carry them home, make mulch.
Mulch that will feed the soil.

I want to pick up all the gumballs
those countless gumballs that fall
from the sweetgum tree. We could
create art together.
I could give you
supplies:
leaves and gumballs,
a cardboard tube.
You can make it yourself.
You can make a masterpiece.
We can be a masterpiece, you and me.

3. Borrowed Lines
Original prompt by Donnetta Norris

Inspiration

Some of Donetta's favorite poems use lines from poems written by other poets. She enjoys discovering lines that speak to her and creating new meanings for the line(s) in her poems. Donnetta's inspiration came from Jennifer Guyor Jowett's Burrows and Seeds (#verselove April 4, 2022). Poets were challenged to "find a seed at the end of [a] piece... and let it serve as a title or beginning line."

Process

For today's poem, borrow a line or lines that resonate with you from a poem shared in class or from your favorite poet. Give the line(s) new meaning by using it in your own poem. Don't forget to give credit to the original poet!

Mentor Poem

"Can We Change Its Course?" by Donnetta Norris

Idle minds
The devil's playground
Idle hands
Lead to poverty
Strong drink
Causes fights
Love of money
Root of evil
Craving money
Pierced with sorrow
People we love
Live life hard
Loved ones pray
Praying hard

The life they choose
Out of control
Ours and Theirs

Can we change its course?
Only God can.

4. Summer Tanka
Original prompt by Sarah J. Donovan

Inspiration

Summer vacation is right around the corner! Sarah asks us to write a poem about the excitement we may have for the promise of summer. You may want to make it silly, thinking about the play that awaits, or you may write in a more serious tone, imagining what fissure it will fill or wound it may heal.

Process

Consider these options: find a picture and describe the scene, describe your favorite summer activity, childhood memories, or use a book as inspiration. Consider writing your poem in *tanka* form, a Japanese verse (similar to the Haiku) with five lines and 31 syllables: 5-7-5-7-7.

- Think of one or two images from your topic and describe them in concrete terms – taste, touch, texture, color, sound. Write that in the first two lines.
- For the third line, state the importance of that moment: all your joy, an escape, pride, comfort, freedom, peace, anxiety, safety, pain. This is a pivot line.
- For the fourth and fifth lines, reflect on what the speaker feels and thinks in this moment: wondering, pondering, asking, hoping, worrying, wishing.
- To test the pivot line, you can flip the first two and the last two lines. It should make sense either way, but you, as the poet, can decide which sequence resonates more.

Mentor Poem

"Take My Hand" by Sarah J. Donovan

Take my hand. Let's climb
the sand dune of rejection,
pushing hurt with toes
kicking up woes. Chin up. Take
the blows with grace, smiles 'pon face.

Reverse Tanka:

Kicking up woes. Chin up. Take
the blows with grace, smiles `pon face.
Pushing hurt with toes,
take my hand. Let's climb
the sand dunes of rejection.

5. The Bop
Original prompt by Mo Daley

Inspiration

Mo was inspired by poet Afaa Michael Weaver's three-stanza-long Bop format. It's simple! Here's the format:

- Stanza 1 is 6 lines long and presents a problem.
- Stanza 2 is 8 lines long and explores or expands the problem.
- Stanza 3 is 6 lines long and presents the solution or shows the failed attempt at resolution.
- Each stanza is followed by a refrain.

You can find more examples at
https://poets.org/glossary/bop

Process

What's on your mind? What issues or problems are taking up head space right now? Jot a quick list. It doesn't matter if the problems are big or small. They may be global or specific to you. Focus on one that you will try to find a solution for, or perhaps have already tried to resolve. Sit down and write! Another possibility might be to incorporate the Bop form into a Problem/Solution lesson and write a whole class Bop.

Mo wrote her poem after her beloved dog was diagnosed with a brain tumor.

Mentor Poem

"Scruffy" by Mo Daley

Old age is hell
especially on those we love
the ones who can't tell us how much pain they are in
if the world is too much with them
if they need us to make the impossible choice
the one we can't bear to make too soon.
How close can we get to the line without crossing it?

The days of fall grow shorter,
so do our days together
the writing on the wall is there,
but I don't want to read it
I've been given too much power—
the decision is too difficult
my heart is torn in two
is it time to say goodbye, or can I have just one more day?
How close can we get to the line without crossing it?

It's agonizing
but as it turns out,
you know. I know.
All that is left is to tearfully say goodbye
and focus on the memories
that will remain long after my tears have dried.
How close can we come to the line without crossing it?

6. Liberation and Joy
Original prompt by Stacey L. Joy

Inspiration

Stacey was inspired to try poet Enta Kusakabe's Gogyohka form. The idea behind the Gogyohka was to take the traditional form of Tanka poetry (which is written in five lines with 5-7-5-7-7 syllable counts), and liberate its structure, creating a freer form of verse. In the 1990s, Kusakabe began his efforts to spread Gogyohka as a new movement in poetry. There are now around half a million people writing this form of verse in Japan.

Process

Today let's write one (5-line free-form poem) or as many Gogyohka poems as we choose. Take a few minutes to focus on liberation and joy. Think of what may bring you joy, what liberates you, or what liberation and joy mean. You might also choose to be inspired by a poem about liberation or joy. Langston Hughes' poem, "Our Land" inspired Stacey's poem.

Mentor Poem

"Joy and Liberation" by Stacey L. Joy

Oh, if this land had the same amount of joy
as popsicle-stained cheeks
and sisters giggling in summer sun,
Earth could unclench her fists
and smile with rainbows.

Oh, if this body could be liberated
on kite string
or butterfly wings,
it would stand naked
in the mirror and shout, "I am free!"

7. 4x4
Original prompt by Denise Krebs

Inspiration

Denise spent some time reflecting on inspirational words about feelings from her favorite poets. How are you and your students feeling today? Joyful, sorrowful, pessimistic, optimistic, alienated, powerful, angry, scared, proud, brave, creative, anxious? What else? Perhaps today you will choose to write about something you cannot accept. Or maybe about the joy of this one wild and precious life. You might write about a feeling you have had recently.

Process

Let's try a 4 x 4 poem today. In this poem, there are four "rules":
- 4 syllables in each line
- 4 lines in each stanza
- 4 stanzas
- Refrain repeated four times in lines 1, 2, 3, 4 of stanzas 1, 2, 3, 4.
- Bonus: Try writing a title in four syllables. There are no rhyming or rhythm restrictions, and you can write on any topic. The 4 x 4 poem is a slight variation of the quatern. It's also similar to the Tricube Poem that Linda Mitchell suggested on ethicalela.com. Alternatively, you might try writing a quatern or tricube.

Mentor Poem

"Day star dawning" by Denise Krebs

Day star dawning
Sunshine beaming
Precious brilliance
Of toasty warmth

Rise in the east
Day star dawning
Warming the earth
With joy and hope

Rising round womb
Growing bundle
Day star dawning
The world awaits

Grandson coming
Family grows
Into sunshine
Day star dawning

8. Why Do You Write Poems?
Original prompt by Andy Schoenborn

Inspiration

Andy writes poetry to laugh, to think, to question, and to express himself. He believes it's a healthy outlet, and one that often traces through memories and hidden emotions. Poetry is where Andy finds himself. By this time of year, students do, too— even, if on the surface, the structure doesn't "look" like poetry.

Andy and his students watch Kyle "Guante" Tran Myhre perform his work "Why Do You Write Poems When Death is All Around Us?" to better understand that poetry can be simple and powerful. All the writer has to do is be willing to listen to the words welling up inside of them.

Process

Find a space to listen to Guante's poem, then have students write their own questions. Begin with "Why do you write poems when...", then answer the question. Continue the next stanza with "Why do you write poems when..." and continue the process until the writer comes to a satisfactory answer.

Mentor Poem

"Why Do You Write Poems When You Could Be Doing Something Constructive?" by Andy Schoenborn

Because I enjoy the company of myself. To tune into my being with nothing but the tap of a keyboard or the scratch of a pen. To dig and scratch away at the inner workings of what has built this life.

Why do you write poems when you could be doing something constructive? Because writing poems *is* constructive. Writing poetry tears down walls. Writing poetry sets the stage. Writing poetry creates a scene. Writing poetry shapes perspectives. Writing poetry builds others up. Writing poetry reveals. With poetry, I tinker and build and repurpose words.

Why do you write poems when you could be doing something constructive? Because my limbs have weakened with time and, yet, my mind is sharp. When my arms are no longer strong enough to hold you I may rely upon my words to wrap you in forgiveness, warmth, and hope. One day you may look back and wonder about me and there I'll be — all of me — written on a page, a scramble of letters, to help you better understand how deeply you were loved.

9. Breaking the Rules
Original prompt by Wendy Everard

Inspiration

Wendy's Creative Writing class listened to poet Ocean Vuong talk about diverging from known paths to forge routes into the Unknown, into new territory. (See his video here.) They considered some literary rule-breakers, and looked at poetry by e.e. cummings, Emily Dickinson, Lewis Carroll, and Gertrude Stein, to the delight of some of Wendy's young writers.

Process

Today, invite students to embrace "breaking the rules" in some way with their poetry. Feel free to break some rules of poetic structure, pushing back at an established form or some rules of grammar or poetry. Or students can write about their relationship to the idea of "breaking the rules" or an experience they've had breaking some. In the Mentor Poem, Mo rearranged cummings' [in Just-] to break her own rules.

Mentor Poem

"Rules" by Mo Daley

cummings broke the RULES, SO why can't i?

when the old puddle-wonderful world
      whistles   wee
Just   in   spring
for the queer balloonman
      jump-rope   and   hop-scotch
          bettyandisabel
            and
                eddieandbill
            come dancing, goat footed
spring piracies
      luscious-mud whistles
Spring is a little lame
and Man!
the balloon-   running wee and   far
     and marbles come
     and it's from the balloonman
     from the world
        and it's
       wee
      and
     far
      and
       whistles

10. Backwards Poetry
Original prompt by Katrina Morison

Inspiration
Katrina was inspired by poet Marwa Helal's immigration journey. Then she discovered, "Poem to Be Read From Right to Left," which is written in a form created by Helal called The Arabic. The Arabic is a form that includes an Arabic letter with an Arabic footnote, and an Arabic numeral, preferably written right to left as the Arabic language is, and vehemently rejects you if you try to read it left to right.

Process

If you are fluent in Arabic, you may strive to follow the Arabic form to the letter. However, the challenge for most of us will be to write a poem from right to left. It is more challenging than you may think. Make the shape of the poem work for you. You could even use rhyme and rhythm for an extra challenge. Play with capitalization and punctuation. For today's theme, try to take on change. Deal with something that is or needs to be turned around. Then, the form will truly reflect the content of the poem. Enjoy!

Mentor Poem

"Piano Practice:" by Rachelle Lipp

ago year one piano playing started I
language new a learning like is notes the reading
to messages sends brain my
pruned it itself of parts
ago decades
instructs teacher patient my
review to me
again Bells Jingle

:right just transition this get never can I
a – in – ride – to is – it – fun – what – Oh
4 X finger second 5 X finger third :hand Right
beats 4 hold finger fifth beats 4 hold finger first :hand Left

backwards it practice to me told she
awhile for
now doing I'm that's so

11. Ode to a Poet
Original prompt by Wendy Everard

Inspiration

Recently Wendy and her daughters visited Emily Dickinson's home in Amherst, Massachusetts, leaving Wendy awestruck. We all have our favorite poets. Wendy counts among hers the English Romantic poets, the aforementioned Miss Emily D, Nikki Giovanni, Amanda Gorman, Charles Bukowski, Clint Smith, Ocean Vuong… and Misha Collins' collection, *Some things I still can't tell you.*

Process

Choose any form that you wish for today's poem – it doesn't have to be a proper "ode" – but your poem must be about, to, or inspired by one of your favorite poets. You can even open it up to favorite writers in any genre, if you'd like. Another option would be to have students write about a classmate who has inspired them with their poetry this year.

Mentor Poem

"Ode to a Poet" by Cara Fortey

Richard Wright, a novel
writer of great renown who
at his life's end found

a fascination
with haiku, four thousand he
wrote in just a year–

his last year–fighting
amoebic dysentery
in his home in France

he studied masters
of the form, publishing eight
hundred seventeen

the mystery is,
will the world ever see the
remaining haikus?

his work was full of
color and strong images–
intriguing haikus

Here are two of his:

Coming from the woods,
a bull has a lilac sprig
dangling from a horn

Their watching faces,
as I walk the autumn road
make me a traveler

12. (Bad)Advice
Original prompt by Scott McCloskey

Inspiration

Reading *Hamlet* with his seniors always allows Scott to spend a bit of time with Polonius's advice to his son, Laertes. Scott would like us to offer "advice" to our fellow poets, students, other teachers, or, really, anyone we interact with. You can even give advice to animals or non-living objects. It's totally up to you! So, let's write some "advice" poems.

BUT WAIT! There's a catch – a small caveat if you will – Scott suggests we only give "bad" advice. Only wrong answers here! Advice can be "good" or "bad" depending on who/what is receiving (or giving) the advice, but don't get caught up in the semantics of it all. Or do. It's up to you. You can "break" the rules a bit as in the mentor poem that actually gives good advice intermixed with the bad.

Process

Scott couldn't find any "Bad Advice Poems" from professional poets, so here are three excellent "Good Advice Poems." Just do the opposite of them. (See? Giving bad advice is easy!) Try Ada Limón's "Instructions on Not Giving Up"; Dan Gerber's "Advice"; and Shane Koyczan's "Instructions for a Bad Day".

Mentor Poem

"Who Says That?" by Denise Hill

Live each day as though it was your last.

I can't imagine worse advice.
No repercussions. No accountability.
Murder. Mayhem. Pillage. Plunder.
Reckless abandonment.
No concern for others.

Seems like enough people already subscribe.

Maybe instead, the advice and tense should be reversed.

Live each day as though it is your first.

13. Monotetra
Original prompt by Tracie McCormick

Inspiration

Tracie's inspiration comes from the **monotetra**, a poetic form developed by Michael Walker. A monotetra poem uses quatrains (four-line stanzas) in tetrameter (four metrical feet) for a total of eight syllables per line. Each quatrain consists of mono-rhymed lines (so each line in the first stanza has the same type of rhyme, as does each line in the second stanza, etc.). The final line of each stanza repeats the same four syllables. This poem can be as short as one quatrain and as long as a poet wishes. Tracie's poem consists of two stanzas, as that seemed to work for her subject.

Process

Oh, the headlines these days! While skimming headlines and trying to decide which to click and read, Tracie saw one called, "Ivanka Trump Called Out By Voters As 'Nepotism Barbie' After She Announces President's New Hiring Order" published by *Hollywood Life by Bonnie Fuller* and written by Jade Boren on June 26, 2020. She was struck by how an order can have a positive or negative impact depending on how it is executed. Thus the subject of this poem was born.

Mentor Poem

"Executive Orders" by Tracie McCormack

Skills-based hiring could be nice.
Since college demands such a price.
Will rich and poor be looked at twice?
Roll of the dice. Roll of the dice.

Barbie earned skills along the way.
Don't use her name without her say.
She's an influencer today.
For more than play. For more than play.

14. Reflections of Hope in My Mother's Eyes
Original prompt by Andy Schoenborn

Inspiration

Andy was inspired by Chilean-American poet Marjorie Agosín's poem "My Mother's Eyes," where the writer shares the hope she sees for herself in the reflection of her mother's eyes. Andy asks us what visions, emotions, experiences, hopes, and dreams might emerge from the reflections of ourselves we find in the eyes of another. What do others see in us that we may not see in ourselves? How might hope spring from those reflections?

Process

Read "My Mother's Eyes" and welcome Agosín's words into the classroom to set the tone for inspiration. Let Marjorie Agosín lead the way. Like Agosín, ask students to begin their poem with "My mother's eyes…" and see where they end up. Or, change out the person: "My friend's eyes…," "My grandfather's eyes…," "My teacher's eyes…," etc. Choose the eyes that inspire hope, peace, grace, joy, or a sense of belonging. Ask students to make intentional choices and consider the effect of those choices readers.

Mentor Poem

"My Mother's Eyes" by Emily Yamasaki

My mother's eyes
are wet rice fields
cut only by the thinnest cement road
skillful taxis daring the edges

My mother's eyes
are neatly lined palm trees
manicured cookie cutter houses
dotting a busy city road

My mother's eyes
are two sets of reds, whites, and blues
divided by a vast
ocean

15. It's All in the Mind
Original prompt by Anna J. Small Roseboro

Inspiration

Anna is a firm believer in the power of positivity. She knows that getting rid of self-sabotaging thoughts can lead to positive changes. Anna asks us to consider locating motivational statements that speak to us. Select three quotations. Use one or more to inspire your writing today.

Process

Using the **pantoum** form, we will summarize in four lines the thoughts evoked by the quotations we read. Then using those four lines as a guide, write twelve more lines following <u>this</u> pattern. Rhyming is encouraged but not required. A pantoum works by repeating lines in a particular order. Have fun.

1. Stanza One: 1, 2, 3, 4
2. Stanza Two: Lines 2, 5, 4, 6.
3. Stanza Three: Lines 5, 7, 6, 8.
4. The final stanza repeats lines in this order: 7, 3, 8, and 1.

Be sure to use quotation marks around any direct quotes.

If students need more scaffolding, there are many pantoum generators online that can make formatting easier.

Mentor Poem

"It's All in the Mind" by Anna J. Small Roseboro

Attitude determines altitude or the height of our flight.
"The only person you are destined to become is the person
you decide to be."
"Whether you think you can or you think you can't,
you're right."
So, it's up to me. Maybe I should just try.

"The only person you are destined to become is the person
you decide to be."
What must I do and who must I ask?
So, it's up to me. Maybe I should just try.
Maybe I'll need help with each and every task.

What must I do and who must I ask?
Admitting I need help is the way to start.
Maybe I'll need help with each and every task.
So, I'll join a group and be a part.

What must I do and who must I ask?
So, I'll join a group and be a part.
"Whether you think you can or you think you can't,
you're right."
Attitude determines the altitude or the height of our flight.

References

Daley, M. (2021, April 2). Bop poem. Ethical ELA. https://www.ethicalela.com/2bop/

Donovan, S. (2019, May 21). Summer tank(a). Ethical ELA. https://www.ethicalela.com/may-summer-tanka-verselove/

Everard, W. (2023, April 9). Breaking the rules. Ethical ELA. https://www.ethicalela.com/breaking-the-rules/

Everard, W. (2023, August 21). Ode to a poet. Ethical ELA. https://www.ethicalela.com/ode-to-a-poet/

Joy, S. (2022, April 13). Liberation and joy. Ethical ELA. https://www.ethicalela.com/liberation-and-joy/

Krebs, D. (2022, April 5). 4 x 4. Ethical ELA. https://www.ethicalela.com/4x4-poem/

McCloskey, S. (2022, October 19). (Bad) advice. Ethical ELA. https://www.ethicalela.com/14183-2/

McCormick, T. (2020, July 21). Monotetra. Ethical ELA. https://www.ethicalela.com/july-openwrite-monotetra/

Morrison, K. (2021, March 17). Backwards poetry. Ethical ELA. https://www.ethicalela.com/backwards-poetry/

Morrison, K. (2023, April 20). A space to look and think. Ethical ELA. https://www.ethicalela.com/?s=space+to+look+

Norris, D. (2023, April 26). Borrowed lines. Ethical ELA. https://www.ethicalela.com/borrowed-lines/

Roseboro, A. (2022, October 15). It's all in the mind. Ethical ELA. https://www.ethicalela.com/its-all-in-the-mind/

Schoenborn, A. (2021, October 19). Reflections of hope in my mother's eyes. Ethical ELA.

https://www.ethicalela.com/reflections-of-hope-in-my-mothers-eyes/

Schoenborn, A. (2023, April 17). Why do you write poems when? Ethical ELA. https://www.ethicalela.com/why-do-you-write-poems-when/

Simon, M. (2023, April 14). Free writing. Ethical ELA. https://www.ethicalela.com/free-writing/

Chapter 8: Concluding and Closure

Dear Teacher,

We hope you are reading this message around April, maybe during spring break because we have some ideas here to help you wrap up your school year in poetic celebrations, and it will take a little bit of planning to do it all justice.

First, good job. We mean it. You have done good. Good for you and your students and the school and beyond. Think about all the poems that exist today because you took the important, intentional step to welcome poetry writing into your teaching practice and curriculum. If your students wrote even 30 poems with you, and if you have about 150 students, then that means there are at least 4500 poems that have been read, written and shared. That means you and your students have been talking about their lives, learning about one another, exploring our communities, walking through the world, and contemplating healing ways of being as part of their education. How fantastic is an education with and through poetry written by students?

So at this point, you will want to know what this has meant for you and your students and consider the next steps on your poetic journey.

We hope you have been including Open Mic (see Chapter 2) for periodic celebrations, and we imagine you may have been inviting students to reflect on their notebooks at the end of each quarter.

In this final chapter, we offer you some ideas for offering optimistic closure for you and your students. Let's begin with this question: What do we do with these notebooks filled with students' poetry?

Culminating Poetry Activities

There are several culminating activities you can do with students at various points throughout the school year or the end of the school year. Below we will list a few:

Class anthology: Below we will say more about portfolios, but you can schedule some time for students to read through their notebooks and put sticky notes on the poems that they want to refine and publish for a class anthology, which can be a digital or physical book. In selecting poems, students may decide they want to feature a new form they created or a poem that explores a topic in a purely metaphoric way that they are pretty proud of. They may think their poem advocating for a social justice issue to be especially important for a larger audience. Invite students to select three or more and then use the Peer Conferring Protocol (see Appendix) for students to revise poems they'd like to contribute to a class anthology. You can create a shared Google doc and assign a few students as editors to be responsible for the formatting. Certainly, you have students who are artists, so they can design the cover and even interior art if you'd like to divide the poems by forms or themes. We suggest you model and teach students how to write a short author bio, and then have a section of the anthology of their names and bios. This makes it professional.

You can leave the anthology in this PDF digital form to share with students and families, or you can move it to a book publishing platform. Amazon, KDP, allows you to publish for free, and students/families can purchase the book for the cost of printing, which is about $5 a copy, depending on the length. There are many other options, too.

The anthology is a wonderful way of honoring the writers in the room and creating a collection of the poems they have shared throughout the year. This is a true representation of the hearts and minds (and words) of your learning community.

Poems on sidewalks: To celebrate writers and their craft, the National Council of Teachers of English has established October

20 as the National Day on Writing®. To celebrate this, Sarah's students wrote lines from their poetry on the sidewalks of their school. You can purchase sidewalk chalk at your local dollar or box store. We recommend you get permission from your school custodian and principal before doing this, and consider the environmental impact of the chalk you choose. Students loved mining their notebooks for their golden lines and then crafting these on the sidewalks. You can do this any time throughout the year when you notice students need to get out of their seats and into the fresh air.

Poems on windows of stores: As an extension of the sidewalk activity and a way to engage the community, we suggest you reach out to your local stores and municipal offices to ask if students can create posters of their poems to hang around the community. You can use Canva or any slides for students to select a favorite poem. Consider places your students and families visit. You can decide the extent to which students will identify themselves. For example, initials or first names may be more appropriate (safe) depending on the age of your students and family preferences.

Poems on cards for family and friends: At various times throughout the year, cards can still be a thing. We know mothers still really appreciate a handwritten card or note from their child -- fathers and guardians, too. And your students may be at the age when they have some feelings of love or crushes. Of course, teacher appreciation is another time of year when a card is welcome. Here we suggest you carve some time -- perhaps when you have an extra day before break-- for students to create some paper or digital cards with their poems or lines from their poems. They can then deliver these to friends, teachers, family members, or even community agencies. Your neighborhood may have a hospital nearby, for example. Students can send poems to the doctors and nurses on Valentine's Day, for taking such good care of patients' hearts.

Lunchtime poetry slams: We wrote about Friday Open Mics in the first chapter. These are class-based, intentional opportunities for students to practice public speaking and listening. However, some students will want more opportunities that are not necessarily connected to assignments or they might want more opportunities to practice reading their poetry. We recommend you offer a school-wide or grade-level month poetry slam during lunch or after school. This need not be a ton of planning -- though you could take it to the next level and create an annual event for the school or district. You can put a sign-up sheet on your door for students to do a public reading of their poems. They can bring their lunch to your class and just do informal readings. Or you can create a rating system so peers can give feedback. We found that the best approach is for two or three students to take the lead on organizing this and setting up the protocols.

Partner with the art and music teachers to create an arts-based showcase: Sarah had a lot of success with the lunchtime poetry slams that some of her students suggested they make a school-wide event. Not every teacher did the daily poetry, but students talked, and students in other classes and grade levels wanted to share their poetry. This morphed into students wanting to sing songs. That was a bit beyond Sarah's expertise, so we contacted the choir director who suggested they bring in the art teacher who was setting up her annual gallery for the open house. Thus, the idea of an arts-based showcase emerged. Sarah, the choir director, and the art teacher collaborated to organize an evening with some refreshments for students to share their art and for parents and community members to come by. We all chipped in with baked goods and coffee, and Sarah created comment cards much like the compliment and listening sheet (see Appendix) for everyone to use so they could write positive celebrations to the arts. We created a wall of envelopes for attendees to put their notes, and then each artist received their envelope at the end. Note: Recruit some especially kind students to help you so that everyone has compliment cards by the end of the evening.

Portfolio Reflection Process

1. First, update the table of contents for your notebook. Then, take some time to read through your notebook.

2. Now, reflect. In a Word document, write a reflection of your notebook and poem writing experiences this semester:
- *Audience:* As you write, consider your audience to be a teacher, friend, peer, and parent interested in hearing about your life as a writer.
- *Genre:* In writing the reflection, format the writing in the genre of a friendly letter, which means a date, greeting, introduction, body, paragraphs, closing, signature, etc.
- *Modality:* In creating the letter, you will mostly use text or the alphabetic mode, but consider including pictures from your notebook as evidence or examples.
- *Task & Craft:* In the body of the letter include the following:
    - Describe your relationship with this notebook this semester as a writer; how did your use evolve, flow (or not), and why -- what forces propelled you to the notebook or from it, etc. over time, how has your perception of writing shifted as a result of keeping this notebook?
    - Which pieces were more enjoyable, moving, and satisfying (which may be the same thing for you and may be different)?
    - What modes (narrative, argument, informational, hybrid), or forms seem to best capture your being or way of thinking or writing style?
    - Did you think about audience or more self-expression or both, and if so how did your writer persona impact your writing?
    - Which is your favorite piece and why: what might be the value or use of Notebooking for you as a teacher or writers?

Student Reflections & Portfolio

While we see portfolios as a culminating activity, we separated this section to unpack the process a bit more. Students benefit from regular reflection so that they can set informed, intentional goals for their learning, so we recommend you carve time for students to do a midterm and end-of-term reflection every semester or so.

Figure 2 Table of contents from student notebook

The first step is to collect and review. Consider this a trip down memory lane. When students look through their **table of contents**, they see what they made; they see the decisions they made. Writers make decisions, and this table of contents is evidence of their writerly self. They can claim the title of writer or poet or whatever they wish.

As students re-encounter their poetry in their notebooks (digital or paper), they may need some modeling from you, the teacher, about the kinds of things they could notice as they now witness their poetry as a collection or an anthology of their own. Perhaps they will want to make a poetry chapbook someday (which could be another culminating activity).

If you have a document camera, we recommend you share your notebook with your students and do some thinking aloud about what you see in your poetry and patterns of your choices. How did your poetry and poetic thinking evolve?

- Perhaps you prefer form poetry but challenged yourself to try some free verse.
- Perhaps you avoided certain topics from your heart, for example, the death of your pet, but later in the year found that you were ready to write about it in the elegy prompt.
- Maybe you found the "Ode to the Unworthy" prompt to be surprising and helped you rethink what poetry is.

- You might talk about the way sharing your poetry impacted your writing. Maybe you have revision marks on a poem after doing a pair-share and can talk about the way a listener helped you see potential in your poem.

Portfolio Table of Contents Spring Semester

	Date	Inspiration	Topic/title	Form	Syntax or technique(s) you are trying/noticing
1	1/20	ungrammatical	when we are closest	free verse	anaphora "when we"
2	1/24	right words	wisdom	haiku	one sentence, enjambment
3	1/25	reality	stress and bees	free verse	gerunds: filling, buzzing, producing
4	1/26	wonderful world	lunar	haiku sonnet	ending with a rhetorical question
5	1/27	re-encountering	prisms	free verse	narrative, I wrote a story
6	1/31	what have you lost	break up	free verse	dialogue and a single scene

- Celebrate a poet in the room who has shaped you and your writing. It is okay (and necessary) to mention how hearing a student's poem about their dog helped you remember your pet.
- You might mention how someone's "Island Earth" poem taught you something new, and you understand poetry to be informative and perhaps more powerful than a 5-paragraph essay. You might point to a poem that you wrote that taught another writer something about the world.

- Perhaps you can say how you feel proud of this work over time and what you discovered about the strength you have developed with regular practice.
- Or maybe you feel more confident talking about poetry because you know and understand the language of form and craft because you used them rather than only studying poetry without actually doing poetry.

After you have done some modeling, your students might be ready to read their poetry and want to share with a peer what they are noticing. Talking through and pointing to poetic moves is eye-opening, and it is a great way to do some pre-writing for the portfolio reflection.

Now, carve some time over the next few days to write about writing poetry. Reflection is learning. It is a synthesis and processing that shows students (and you, the teacher) what transformations have come. Below is the **Portfolio Reflection** Sarah used in her junior high and college classes.

Teacher Reflection

Now that you have modeled your reflection as a poet and have witnessed the reflections of your students, you can take some time to think about your pedagogical content knowledge of poetry. Ideally, you and a colleague have engaged in this year's poetry, so you can do some of this reflection (and planning for next year) together. This is thinking about all you have learned about poetry and about teaching poetry and about teaching poets; this is time for re-articulating what *writing* poetry means and can do, specifically, in your school and community context.

So what, dear teacher-poet, have you learned?

- *Identity:* Has your identity as an English language arts teacher changed in any way?
- *Skills:* What have you learned about writing prompts and what works for whom and when? What have you

learned about moving students into and out of writing experiences?

- *Community:* What have you learned about supporting students as peer-writers? What have you learned about building community? What do you see in the ways everyone interacts that might be poetic being? Have you noticed or has poetry surfaced harm and healing for greater wellbeing? What adjustments did you have to make to nurture safe spaces for writing?
- *Routines:* What you are learning about the value of routines, continuity,
- *Content:* What do you understand about writing and poetry that you may not have understood last year? What do you still need to learn or find that you want to learn more about?
- *Forward-thinking:* What ideas do you have for next year? What prompts might you keep or change? What moves will you make to support, scaffold, encourage, and nurture safety? Were there prompts that fell flat and might need a new mentor poem or some tweaking? Probably. You can revise these. Will life and world issues make new prompts necessary?

Concluding Thoughts

As you reflect on the incredible journey of integrating poetry into your classroom, take a moment to celebrate the profound impact it has had on you and your students. From the thousands of poems that have been written and shared to the deep conversations and connections forged through this creative process, you have cultivated an enriching educational experience that goes beyond traditional learning. Your dedication to fostering a poetic environment has not only honed your students' writing skills but also nurtured their emotional and social growth. As you consider the next steps on this poetic journey, remember to cherish these moments of creativity and connection. Whether it's through class anthologies, sidewalk poetry, community engagements, or reflective portfolios, the legacy of your poetic endeavors will continue to inspire and uplift your students. Here's to the future of poetry in your classroom and the countless new voices waiting to be heard.

Thank you for taking us along with you on this journey.

Peace,
Sarah, Mo, & Maureen

Appendix

Table of Forms

Students can paste this into their notebooks so they can try different poems as they are inspired to do so. They can also use this table to imagine their own form, drawing on various features from a range of options.

Form	Stanza	Lines	Meter/ Syllable	Typical Topic	Rhyme Scheme	Pattern of Repetition
4X4	4	4	4	any	no	The first line is repeated 4 times in lines 1, 2, 3, and 4 of each stanza.
acrostic	varied	varied	consistent	any	no	Relies on the repetition of initial letters to convey a message related to the word those letters form
The Arabic	any	any	any	any	any	Write the poem from right to left
blackjack	1 or more	3	7	any	no	Uses enjambment; typically one complex sentence; can be repeated to tell a story
blitz	1	50	short	any	no	Intense and quick progression, each line begins with the last word of the previous line; no punctuation
bop	3	6-10	varies	personal or social issues	yes	ABAB - CDCD - E includes refrain

Form	Stanza	Lines	Meter/ Syllable	Typical Topic	Rhyme Scheme	Pattern of Repetition
cinquain	1	5	2-4-6-8-2	any	no	There is a merging then a topic switch in line 6 (see didactic and American within the chapter)
decima	1	10	varies	any	yes	ABBAACCDDC or ABBAACCDDC
diamante	1	7	word count	two objects	no	Involves a pattern of words, progressing from one subject to another
duplex	1	14	couplets	any	yes	AB bC cD dE eF like the sonnet and ghazal; the second line (or some variation of the couplet becomes the first line of the next couplet
elegy	any	any	any	grief, death	no	Reflecting on a person or something that died
etheree	1	10	incremental	any	no	Match the syllable count to the line line 1, 1 syllable
extended haiku	varies	3s	5-7-5	any	no	Multiple haiku that work together to explore a topic in multiple ways or as a narrative
ghazal	5-15	couplets	same meter per line	loss, mysticism, love	yes	AA BA CA and so on, the second line of each couplet rhymes; repeated rhyming word

Form	Stanza	Lines	Meter/ Syllable	Typical Topic	Rhyme Scheme	Pattern of Repetition
Gogyohka	1	5	5-7-5-7-7	any	no	Liberating the structure and themes of haiku and tanka
gogyoshi	1	5	varies	any	no	Concise expression
haiku	1	3	5-7-5	nature	no	A pivot from observation to aha
hay(na)ku	1	3	varies	any	no	First line has one word; second has 2 words, third has 3 words
lazy sonnet	1	14	one word	any	yes	ABAB CDCD EFEF GG
monotetra	1	4	8	any	yes	AAAa, with the fourth line using the rhyme of the preceding 3 lines
nocturn	varies	varies	varies	night, darkness, contemplative	varies	includes repeated images or themes
nonet	1	9	incremental	any	no	Start at 9 syllables in line 1 and decrease to 1 syllable in line 1
pantoum	multiple	4 per stanza	consistent	any	yes	ABAB, each line is repeated in a specific pattern for a weaving effect
rondeau	3	8 or 10	varies	love, nature, light themes	yes	ABbaabAB with capital letters indicating repeated lines

Form	Stanza	Lines	Meter/ Syllable	Typical Topic	Rhyme Scheme	Pattern of Repetition
skinny	1	11	word count	any	yes	The 1st and 11th line are the same words rearranged; lines 2-6-10 repeat single words; other lines are single words, too
sonnet	1	14	10	love	yes	ABAB CDCD EFEF GG
tanka	1	5	5-7-5-7-7	nature, humanity	no	A pivot line that shifts focus or tone
tricube	1	3	3 -3-3	any	no	Syllable count
tritina	3	9	10	any	yes	ABC, CAB, BCA, end words of the lines repeating in a specific pattern

Glossary of Terms

This is another resource that students can paste into their notebooks. We imagine many are familiar to students already, but there may be some new ones. Again, students may want to check off which ones they try or play with during the school year and refer back to this list to develop their repertoire of craft moves. to paste in notebooks.

Term	Definition
Alliteration	The repetition of the same consonant sounds at the beginning of words that are in close proximity.
Allusion	A brief and indirect reference to a person, place, thing, or idea of historical, cultural, literary, or political significance.
Anaphora	The repetition of a word or phrase at the beginning of successive clauses or lines.
Enjambment	The continuation of a sentence or clause across a line break in a poem, without a pause or punctuation.
Figurative Language	Language that uses figures of speech, such as similes, metaphors, allusions, personification, hyperbole, oxymoron, anthropomorphism, and apostrophe.
Form	The structure and organization of a poem, including its length, stanza arrangement, rhyme scheme, and meter.
Hyperbole	An exaggerated statement not meant to be taken literally, used for emphasis or effect.
Imagery	Descriptive language that appeals to the senses, creating vivid mental pictures for the reader.

Term	Definition
Innovative	Writing that is unexpected or non-cliché, often involving a fresh approach to form, structure, or conclusion.
Jargon	Discipline or content-specific language that shows expertise or knowledge in a particular field.
Logos	Persuasion through logic, using facts, details, examples, research, reasoning, and explanations.
Metaphor	A figure of speech that directly compares two unlike things by stating that one is the other.
Meter	The rhythmic structure of a poem, determined by the pattern of stressed and unstressed syllables in each line.
Onomatopoeia	A word that phonetically imitates the sound it describes, such as "buzz" or "sizzle."
Pathos	Persuasion by appealing to the audience's emotions, using powerful phrases or ideas to evoke feelings such as disgust, sadness, joy, laughter, urgency, or compassion.
Personification	A figure of speech where human characteristics are attributed to non-human things or abstract ideas.
Repetition	The deliberate use of the same word or phrase multiple times in a text to create emphasis or rhythm.
Repetition (General)	The act of repeating words, phrases, or structures for emphasis, including forms like anaphora, epistrophe, asyndeton, polysyndeton, analepsis, alliteration, assonance, and consonance.
Rhyme Scheme	The pattern of rhymes at the end of each line of a poem, typically described using letters to denote which lines rhyme.

Term	Definition
Sensory Language	Descriptive language that appeals to the senses (smell, sound, taste, touch, sight) to create vivid imagery and bring the setting or characters to life.
Simile	A figure of speech comparing two unlike things using "like" or "as."
Stanza	A grouped set of lines in a poem, often separated by a space, that usually follows a specific pattern of meter and rhyme.
Syntax	The arrangement of words and phrases to create well-formed sentences, including varied sentence structures such as gerunds, infinitives, subordinating conjunctions, asyndeton, anaphora, parentheticals, appositives, and parallelism.
Transitions	Words or phrases that show changes in time, place, or ideas, including subordinating conjunctions (when, while, after, before) and conjunctive adverbs (thus, however, therefore).
Translanguaging	The process of using multiple language varieties in a single conversation or text, allowing speakers to draw on their entire linguistic repertoire.

VEEPPP: Public Speaking Guide

Students can paste this into their notebooks for reminders about how to read aloud and perform their poem (or other writing) in a more formal setting like the open mic.

VEEPP	Public Speaking
Volume	We can hear you in the back of the room. You may make your voice louder or softer in certain parts to emphasize something, show passion/emotion, or make the audience lean in, but it is related to content. Your volume does not distract from your message.
Eye Contact	We can see your eyes at different points of the performance to show you are trying to connect with us – your audience. You can hold eye contact with 3 angles of the room, so you are showing you know your content well.
Expression	The way you say the words and phrases shows you are interpreting the mood and content to communicate to the audience. You may change expression in different parts as the mood shifts or ideas become more serious or light-hearted.
Pace	You stay within the time allowed. You perform with a pace that matches the content and mood; it is slow enough for us to hear and process the words and fast enough for us to feel the rhythm. You may slow down to emphasize certain parts or to let an important idea really resonate with the audience.
Pronunciation	You practiced and know the words you've written, especially technical ones. The audience is not distracted by phrasing or unclear pronunciation.
Professionalism	You prepared for the performance. You stand strong (no swaying), say "thank you" at the end to signal closure, stay for a moment to accept the applause, and your demeanor treat the topic and audience with respect.

Two-Voice Template

Students write with a partner -- someone perhaps they haven't yet spoken to this school year (and may not know their name). Paste this chart in their notebooks and have them talk through each line. Feel free to skip lines or revise them. Choose categories for the poem from this (add others as you wish): Books, Artists, Musicians, Social media, Plays, Genres, Movies, Writing, Poetry, Activities, Costumes, Clothes, Technology, and Games.

Topic	Name	Name
I am from (choose category and list a few), (further description)		
From (choose another category and list two of a category)		
I am from (describe how you do/consume one of the categories)		
From (something you learned about life from one of the categories)		
I am from (a category that may work as a metaphor for who you are or that has shaped who you are)		
From (a category that you used to escape/feel seen/another verb and how)		
The (another detail of a category), (its impact on you, why it mattered)		
From (a specific event, story, time that you engaged in that category)		
I'm from (another detail of a category that is important to you that may sum it all up)		

Listening Handout

Listener's Name: _____

Something to celebrate about the author's writing!

- o **Jargon:** discipline or content-specific language: fancy words and words specific to the subject/topic (shows expertise/knowledge)
- o **Figurative language:** simile, metaphor, allusion, personification, hyperbole, oxymoron, anthropomorphism, apostrophe
- o **Repetition:** anaphora, epistrophe, asyndeton, polysyndeton, analepsis, alliteration, assonance, consonance
- o **Sensory language:** smell, sound, taste, touch, sight -colors, shapes, textures, movement -- the setting/place comes alive, can imagine characters
- o **Logos:** facts, details, examples, research, reasoning, explanations, logic
- o **Pathos:** emotional, powerful phrases/ ideas that cause disgust, sadness, joy, laughter, sense of urgency, outrage, compassion, sympathy
- o **Innovative:** unexpected lead, twist, ending, non-cliche; form: inserting an epistle, poem, mixing genre forms; the conclusion was fresh (something we haven't heard)
- o **Transitions:** subordinating conjunctions (when, while, after, before) show time/place/idea changes; conjunctive adverbs (thus, however, therefore, on one hand, on the other hand)
- o **Syntax:** starting with a gerund, infinitive, subordinating conjunction, asyndeton, anaphora, parentheticals, appositives, parallelism; long, short, one-word sentences.

Name	Feature to Celebrate	Text Evidence Check if you complimented the author.→	
Sarah	Sensory language -- **smell**	"rotting stench of a fish left in the garbage for days"	❑
			❑
			❑
			❑

Compliment Giving (look at the person): *(Name), when you read, "QUOTE," I thought it was a (vivid, effective, thoughtful, creative, innovative, moving, brave) example of (TECHNIQUE) because (REASON).*

> Example: *Julie, when you read, "rotting stench of a fish left in the garbage for days," I thought it was a powerful example of sensory language because fish in the garbage is offensive and lingers.*

Compliment Receiving (look at the person): *Thank you* (looking at the person.)

Peer Conferring Protocol

Peer Conferring Protocol for the Writer

Writer's Name:_____
Listeners' Name(s): #1_____ &
#2_____

Instructions: Before you read or ask for feedback let your listener know what you need from them: *One thing I really want your feedback on is (my opening, closing, organization, transition, etc.).*

Now, read your writing to the listener. If you notice anything you'd like to change as you read, feel free to stop and make that revision.

When you are done reading, ask the listen some questions and write notes of their responses to help you with your revisions:

    4. What stood out to you as a reader/listener?
#1
#2

    5. What feedback do you have based on my initial request?
#1
#2

    6. What are you still wondering about, would like to hear more about, or would you like me to make more clear/or less obvious in my revision?
#1
#2

Thank the listeners. Invite them to share their writing with you.

Bonus Poems

Writers seem to know where to go for inspiration — nature, art, photographs, books, poetry, authors, memory. But when a writer is faced with an empty page or a flashing cursor, a writer's mind can go blank and, along with it, any sense of hope that the words will come.

Indeed, sometimes what a writer needs the most is another writer — for their inspiration, for their process, for their mentor text. And so, Ethical ELA offers teachers and students a collection of writers (and their prompts) to keep writing alive.

The 50 ways offered here are merely suggestions — not rules. In a writer's world, a suggestion is an invitation to play with the idea, stretch into new ways of seeing the word and the world (Freire), express dormant emotions or silenced perspectives, and even disrupt standardized words, syntax, and form by inventing new words, fracturing expectations, and inventing forms. Sometimes rejecting a suggestion is just that sense of power a writer needs to tackle the waiting cursor.

Teachers, you are welcome to write with us each month at www.ethicalela.com for our Open Write (find out more on the website) and follow the site, Instagram, and YouTube for poetry prompts to share with your students throughout the year. If you loop with your students, you will especially want to keep adding to and modifying prompts that work for your students, their community, and the goings on of the world. Enjoy.

50 More Ways of Community
1. Origin Stories
2. Giving Voice
3. Synesthesia & Color
4. Aural Textures
5. Epistolary
6. Dramatic Monologue
7. Wonder Women
8. Bop Poem
9. Echo Sonnet

About the Authors

Sarah J. Donovan is a former junior high English language arts teacher of fifteen years and an Associate Professor of Secondary English Education at Oklahoma State University. She has edited two other collections of poetry: *Rhyme & Rhythm: Poems for Student Athletes* and *Teacher-Poets Writing to Bridge the Distance.*

Mo Daley is a mostly retired middle school reading specialist living in the suburbs of Chicago. She enjoys reading, writing, birdwatching, hiking, and traveling. Mo keeps busy with literacy outreach programs locally and globally. But more than anything, Mo enjoys spending time with her family.

Maureen Young Ingram lives and writes in Silver Spring, Maryland. Now retired, she taught preschool and mentored adults in their work with young children. Maureen loves spending time with her two granddaughters, hiking, and gardening. She enjoys writing poetry and is immensely grateful for the Ethical ELA writing community.

Featured Poets

We'd like to introduce you to the featured poets in this collection (in alphabetical order by first names). They are great teacher-friends to add to your writing professional development network.

Allison Berryhill lives in Iowa where she advises the journalism program, teaches English, and hosts a weekly Creative Writing club at Atlantic High School. She is active with the Iowa Council of Teachers of English, the Iowa High School Press Association, and the Iowa Poetry Association where she serves as a teacher liaison. Allison is a runner, an accordion player, and a wedding officiant. Follow her at @allisonberryhil for photos of #IowaSky and schoolblazing.blogspot.com for random musings.

Amber Harrison lives in Grove, OK, where she teaches English Language Arts at Grove High School. She serves as the sponsor for the International Club: this past summer, Amber traveled with students on adventures across Japan; and this upcoming summer they will go to Venice, The Alps, and Paris. Amber is also an instructional coach for the First Class Teacher Induction Program – virtually engaged in coaching cycles and conversations on classroom management and instructional practice with second- and third-year teachers across Oklahoma. Amber promotes life-long learning for all people.

Amy Vetter is an associate professor in English education in the School of Education at the University of North Carolina Greensboro, where she teaches undergraduate courses in teaching practices and curriculum of English and literacy in the content area, and graduate courses in youth literacies, teaching research, and qualitative research design. Her areas of research are literacy and identity, the writing lives of youth, and critical conversations. She co-directs a young writers' camp at UNCG in the summer. Before her job in higher education, she taught all levels of tenth and twelfth-grade English in Austin, Texas. Amy lives in Greensboro with her husband and two daughters. When she's not in the classroom, you'll probably find her running, cycling, hiking, or reading a book.

Andy Schoenborn is an award-winning author and high school English teacher in Michigan at Clare Public Schools. He focuses his work on progressive literacy methods including student-centered critical thinking, digital collaboration, and professional development. He is a past-president of the Michigan Council of Teachers of English, Vice President for the Michigan Reading Association, and Teacher Consultant for the Chippewa River Writing Project. His first book, co-authored with Dr. Troy Hicks, Creating Confident Writers was published in 2020. Follow him on Twitter @aschoenborn.

Angie Braaten has been teaching English Language Arts since 2013. She started her teaching career in Louisiana for five years, then moved overseas and taught in Bangladesh and Kuwait. Her overseas experiences have opened her mind in ways that may have never happened if she had stayed in the states. She has experience teaching grades 6-11 but her favorite would probably be 8th, a grade that will always hold a special place in her own heart, for reasons you will learn in her poem today! She is grateful for this community of writers who have taught her so much and to have monthly opportunities to write, read, and share poetry.

Anna J. Small Roseboro is a wife and mother, poet and writing coach, and National Board Certified Teacher with over forty years of experience. She has taught English and Speech to students in middle school, high school, and Literacy in the Content Areas and Curriculum Design to students in college, in public, parochial, and private schools in five states. She now is directing her attention to online ministries, coaching new writers, and mentoring early career classroom teachers in middle schools, high schools, and colleges. She has self-published books in various genres. Rowman Littlefield Education has published ten of Anna's textbooks for teachers. Anna has been an active member of this writing community for several years and eagerly joins the conversations each month. Poems she has written in OPEN WRITE have been published in multiple publications, including BRIDGE THE DISTANCE: An Oral History of COVID-19 in Poems (2020) and RHYME & RHYTHM: Poems for Student Athletes (2021).

Barbara Edler has taught English for the last forty years in IA, the last thirty in Keokuk where she encouraged students to find their voice while taking risks, coaching speech participants, and supporting NHD competitors. During the last few years of teaching, Barb worked with talented and gifted students and honed her technology and engineering skills. Keokuk is located in the very southeast tip of the state where she enjoys watching the Mississippi roll by, reading, writing, playing cards, watching birds, and appreciating the simple things in life.

Betsy Jones lives and teaches in Moultrie, GA. In her ninth year as a full-time teacher, Betsy is currently an Academic Coach and 7th grade ELA Remote Learning teacher; she has taught Literature/Composition and Drama to 9th through 11th graders. Before accepting the call to become a teacher, she supervised tutoring programs in California; waited tables in South Georgia cafes; mentored students for high school graduation; taught English in Tegucigalpa, Honduras; and managed an independent bookstore. She is a life-long reader, writer, and self-professed "word nerd."

Britt Decker lives in Houston, TX, where she writes, reads, laughs, and learns alongside brilliant 10th graders. She began participating in writing communities in 2020 and has discovered the powerhouse poets of the monthly Open Writes. When Britt isn't in the classroom or writing in her notebook, you can find her drinking black coffee and discussing educational inequities with her husband while simultaneously wrangling her two toddlers.

Bryan Ripley Crandall lives in Stratford, CT, where he directs the Connecticut Writing Project and is Associate Professor of English Education at Fairfield University. He gained his teaching legs at the J. Graham Brown School in Louisville, Kentucky, a K-12 public school with a mission for diversity, inclusivity, and equity, and currently brings a love of verse to award-winning Young Adult Literacy Labs and teacher institutes. He is co-host of National Writing Project's The Write Time.

Cara Fortey lives in Salem, OR, where she is in her 26th year at South Salem High School. She teaches World Literature and Philosophy, Creative Writing, Creative Writing 2, and remedial reading. She spends her free time with her two sons (ages 19 and 16) and Maté, her Goldendoodle.

Darius Phelps is a doctoral student at Teachers College, Columbia University. He is an adjunct professor at CUNY Queens, Hunter College, Teachers College, and intern at Brooklyn Poets. An educator, poet, spoken word artist, and activist, Darius writes poems about grief, liberation, emancipation, reflection through the lens of a teacher of color and experiencing Black boy joy. His poems have appeared in the NY English Record, NCTE English Journal, Pearl Press Magazine, and ëëN Magazine's The 2023 Valentine Issue. Recently, he was featured on WCBS and highlighted the importance of Black male educators in the classroom.

Denise Hill lives in the small town of Bay City, MI, which is not on a bay. Go figure. She is winding down thirty-some-years of two-year college teaching where she poured her heart and soul into breaking down barriers in higher education for developmental writers – until legislators and administrators decided too much help isn't a good thing and essentially ended that career. But she's not bitter. Much. She still enjoys teaching comp and world mythology and has redirected her energies into editing NewPages.com, an online resource promoting literary magazines, small presses, indie bookstores, and creative writing programs. She uses early mornings to walk, read, write, art, and yoga and looks forward to hanging out with friends on Ethical ELA every month.

Denise Krebs has been writing poetry with students for decades, but she has enjoyed several years with this dynamic and encouraging poetry-writing community of Verselove at Ethical ELA. Denise has a master's degree in elementary education with a concentration in teaching reading. Now in her final year in Bahrain, she has become a volunteer reading interventionist at her school–the first modern school in Bahrain, which started in 1899. She is enjoying more time to cook, bake, create, write, tell stories, and get ready for retirement in California. Follow her on Twitter at @mrsdkrebs. She blogs at Dare to Care. She co-authored The Genius Hour Guidebook, published by Routledge Eye on Education and Middle Web, now in the second edition.

Donnetta Norris is a 2nd grade teacher in Arlington, TX. She has facilitated writing and blogging workshops with TeachWrite, LLC. She is one of the writing sessions for TeachWrite's, Time To Write as well. She has been a guest blogger with Teach Better Team. You can read much of her writing on TeacherReaderWriter, The Rogue Scholar, and Writing Is A Journey. She is a published poet in Teacher-Poets Writing to Bridge the Distance: An Oral History of COVID-19 in Poems by Dr. Sarah J. Donovan. Follow her on Twitter at @NorrisDonnetta.

Emily Cohn lives in Vinalhaven, ME, an island 15 miles from the mainland, where she teaches middle schoolers science and ELA at the Vinalhaven School. Emily believes in student voice and choice, and making connections to our world. She received recognition from Maine Environmental Education Association as an innovative educator. She spends her free time with her husband and 4-month-old son, walking and looking for tiny things.

Emily Yamasaki lives in San Diego, CA, where she teaches at San Diego Global Vision Academy. She serves as a teacher leader and instructional coach at her site, creating and presenting professional development for the teaching team. Emily is also a fellow and teacher-consultant with the San Diego Area Writing Project under the National Writing Project. As a teacher consultant, she is honored to work with a diverse teacher and student population across San Diego. Emily believes in teachers teaching teachers and strives to perpetuate that model. She spends her free time with her husband, 3-year-old son, and rescue dog.

Erica Johnson lives in the suburbs of Little Rock, AR, while teaching in the rural town of Vilonia. She has dedicated a dozen years to helping juniors and seniors earn college credit for English. Erica is currently improving her teaching game by attending Arkansas Leadership Academy. This decision came out of the work she does as part of the writing community called Teach Write and the Teach Write Academy. Erica spends her non-writing time in the company of her "grumpy old man" dog, Cooper, or setting new personal records at her local CrossFit gym.

Genevieve McCalla is an AHS senior and a second-year editor for AHS Needle. McCalla enjoys doing cross country, tennis, choir, show choir, jazz choir, the play, the musical, speech, debate, NHS, and first Fridays. Allison Berryhill is her teacher.

Glenda Funk retired from full-time teaching in 2019 after a 38-year career and is now substitute teaching in her district. In addition to being a dog and cat mom, Glenda loves to travel and is a doting grandmother to Ezra, who at 22 months loves board books and is learning numbers, colors, and ABCs with Mom. Glenda was recently invited to be on the NCTE Children's Poetry Awards Committee and is serving a three-year term. Glenda is participating in the Stafford Poetry Challenge to write a poem a day for a year. Glenda blogs at Swirl & Swing: www.glendafunk.wordpress.com

Jennifer Guyor Jowett, middle-grade ELA instructor, *Into the Shadows* author, Dog Eared Book Awards creator, word celebrator, mitten state dweller, and classroom innovator.

Jessica Wiley lives in Conway, AR, aka, "The City of Roundabouts". An educator for 14 years, for the past two years she has taught in an alternative learning environment. One of the many passions in her life is advocacy for appropriate, educational, and functional services and programs for children with special needs. She is an avid reader a lover and a writer of poetry. She is married with an 11-year-old daughter and an 8-year-old son.

Jordan Stamper lives in Suffolk, VA, where she teaches at Nansemond-Suffolk Academy, an independent, collegiate preparatory school, where she teaches advanced junior English classes and a creative writing elective. After spending six years in diverse public schools in Houston, TX, she has the privilege of cultivating the love of reading and writing by utilizing more creative means. Jordan spends her free time with her husband and two young daughters while trying to continue to write for herself.

Judi Opager works at a Middle School in Torrance, CA. Her first love is her students. She is a contributing member of The Poetry Society of America. Like most poets, she discovered her writing talent at an early age, heralding the woes of Arithmetic in her 1960 fourth-grade class. She credits her poetry for keeping her sane in some fairly insane times. She has an ongoing discussion with her followers on @doorwaystothefuture and has begun her poetry website at: https://www.judiopager.com/

Katalyn Wiley is Jessica's daughter in middle school.

Katrina Morrison lives in Tulsa, OK. A tenth-grade English teacher, she is a firm believer in the frequent use of mentor texts whether written by her, one of her students, or someone from the world outside. Her students know she is passionate about poetry too. She sneaks it in whenever she gets the chance. April's #VerseLove has been a refuge for her since the most difficult days of the pandemic in 2020.

Kim Johnson, Ed.D., lives in Williamson, GA, where she serves as District Literacy Specialist for Pike County Schools. She enjoys writing, reading, traveling, and spending time with her husband and three rescue schnoodles – Boo Radley (TKAM), Fitz (F. Scott Fitzgerald), and Ollie (Mary Oliver). You can follow her blog, Common Threads: patchwork prose and verse, at www.kimhaynesjohnson.com.

Laura Langley teaches English to 11th and 12th graders at an Arts/Music Magnet in Little Rock, AR.

Leilya Pitre lives in Ponchatoula, LA, which is known as the Strawberry Capital of the World. She teaches at Southeastern Louisiana University and coordinates the English Education Program. As a teacher educator, she is passionate about helping her students to become nourishing, devoted, and effective teachers in the classrooms. She is one of the co-editors of Study and Scrutiny: Research on Young Adult Literature and one of the curators of Dr. Bickmore's YA Wednesday Weekend Picks. She loves to learn about people, cultures, and rich traditions all over the world. In her free time, she reads, writes, listens to music, visits her children and grandchildren, or travels with her husband.

Linda Mitchell is a family girl, a Middle School Librarian, creative, curious, and loves learning! Find her poems in Rhyme and Rhythm (Archer. 21) Celebrating Ten in Ten Different Ways (wee words for wee ones '21) and, Teacher-Poets Writing to Bridge the Distance (OSU Libraries. 21). She keeps a weekly commitment to Poetry Friday blogging at A Word Edgewise and invites you to learn more about participating in Poetry Friday at: https://www.nowaterriver.com/what-is-poetry-friday/ .

Margaret Simon lives on the Bayou Teche in New Iberia, LA. Margaret has been an elementary school teacher for 36 years, most recently teaching gifted students in Iberia Parish. Her first book of children's poetry was published in 2018 by UL Press, *Bayou Song: Creative Explorations of the South Louisiana Landscape.* Margaret's poems have appeared in anthologies including *The Poetry of US* by National Geographic and *Rhyme & Rhythm: Poems for Student Athletes.* Margaret writes a blog regularly at http://reflectionsontheteche.com.

Maureen Young Ingram lives and writes in Silver Spring, MD. Now retired, she taught preschool and mentored adults in their work with young children. Maureen loves spending time with her two granddaughters, hiking, and gardening. She blogs regularly at maureenyoungingram.blogspot.com and enjoys writing poetry about children, family, and nature. Maureen is immensely grateful for the Ethical ELA writing community.

Melanie Crowder is the acclaimed author of several books for young readers. She writes YA novels: Audacity, An Uninterrupted View of the Sky, Mazie, and Jumper. She also writes middle-grade novels of all sorts: Three Pennies, A Nearer Moon, Parched, and the duology The Lighthouse between the Worlds and A Way between Worlds. She recently published her first picture books: *Great Gusts* and *Sea Wolves*. Melanie teaches writing at Vermont College of Fine Arts and lives under the big blue Colorado sky with her family.

Mo Daley is a mostly retired middle school reading specialist living in the suburbs of Chicago. She enjoys reading, writing, birdwatching, hiking, and traveling. Mo keeps busy with literacy outreach programs locally and globally. But more than anything, Mo enjoys spending time with her family.

With a relationships-first attitude, **Rachelle Lipp** has learned a lot in nearly a decade of teaching high school English. A voracious reader, hopeful poet, and learner, she has led professional development on inquiry-based learning, presented ways to make Shakespeare fun at a state-wide conference, and engaged students daily through culturally relevant lesson planning.

Ruth Reneau is a teacher at E.P. Yorke High School in Belize City, Belize.

Sarah J. Donovan is a former junior high English language arts teacher of fifteen years and an Assistant Professor of Secondary English Education at Oklahoma State University.

From Monroe, MI, Scott McCloskey has been teaching English language arts at the secondary level for nearly 30 years and as a part-time adjunct at a community college for 20 years. When not in the classroom, he enjoys reading and writing and spending time with his wife. He writes (and reads) poetry because he has yet found no better way to understand himself or humanity than by reading and writing poetry.

Seana Hurd Wright is from Los Angeles, CA. Seana has been teaching for 30 years primarily in the Elementary sector. She is a National Board Certified Teacher and has taught all grades yet prefers upper grades. She has been fascinated with writing since Middle School and wrote a soap opera-ish novel with a friend in 7th grade that was silly yet exhilarating. Writing has always been natural and easy for her and she's grateful to be able to share her thoughts in this anthology.

Sheri Vasinda hails from Texas where she taught K-4 students and especially enjoyed following student questions that led to finding out about the insides of water towers and how they work, the possible makeup of black holes, the viciousness of hippopotami, and the life of our school's namesake (Chester Story). She was a reading/literacy specialist focused on finding literacy talents. She currently lives in Stillwater, OK, and teaches literacy education courses at Oklahoma State University. She is curious about people, places, and possibilities. She and her husband Mark love visiting their grown children and grandchildren and other interesting places.

Stacey L. Joy, a native of Los Angeles, CA, has been an elementary school teacher for 35 years. Stacey is a National Board Certified Teacher and currently teaches multiple subjects in 5th grade. She received her bachelor's degree from U.C.L.A. and her master's degree from C.S.U.D.H. Stacey has been writing poetry most of her life but being a fellow of the U.C.L.A. Writing Project helped her connect her writing with her teaching practice.

Stefani Boutelier, Ph.D. is an Associate Professor of Education at Aquinas College in Grand Rapids, MI. Most of her K-12 classroom teaching was at the secondary level in Southern California but she has worked at all levels of education for nearly 20 years. Her published works are in both academic and creative genres.

Susie Morice, writer and editor, is a consultant with Santa Fe Center for Transformational School Leadership and the Institute for School Partnership at Washington University in St. Louis. Susie is also a Teacher-Consultant with The Gateway Writing Project, a former public school classroom teacher for 30 years, and a poet, who is the winner of Member-at-Large Best Poem, 2014 – Missouri State Poetry Society contest.

Tammi Belko is a 5th and 6th grade ELA teacher and Gifted Intervention Specialist. As a middle school teacher and Power of the Pen writing coach, Tammi has spent over fifteen years sharing her love of reading, writing and poetry with her students. Tamara lives in a suburb of Cleveland, OH, with her husband and three children. When she isn't absorbed in reading young adult literature, she can be found listening to music with her family, enjoying a walk or learning Tai Chi. She is the author of the young adult verse novel, *Perchance to Dream*.

Tammy Breitweiser lives in Beloit, WI, where she is a literacy coach in the School District of Beloit. In her spare time, she teaches writing classes. Over her 26 years in education, she has been a classroom teacher, reading specialist, TAP Master Teacher, and coach. She believes reading is the gateway to everything. You can find her on IG @inspiretammyb or at her website https://tammysreadinglife.wordpress.com/.

Tracie McCormick holds master's degrees in English and school leadership and teaches ELA and social studies in Oak Forest, IL. Her one word this year is ATTEMPT, so she is enjoying new methods of personal and professional growth, which is what led her to ethicalela.com. Follow her on Twitter at @TracieMcTeacher.

In gratitude...

A very special thank you to all the teachers and families who nurture the hearts and minds of writers so that they can be, now and in the future, our storytellers and poets.

ALSO AVAILABLE
FROM ETHICAL ELA CONTRIBUTORS

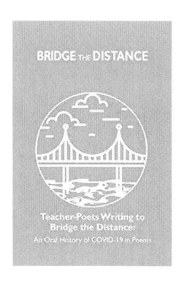

Made in the USA
Columbia, SC
02 September 2024

41491552R00167